NO BULL INVESTING

Straightforward Advice
to Maximize Your Returns in Any Market,
with Any Amount of Money

JAKE BERNSTEIN

Dearborn™
Trade Publishing
A **Kaplan Professional** Company

Vice President and Publisher: Cynthia A. Zigmund
Senior Managing Editor: Jack Kiburz
Interior Design: Lucy Jenkins
Cover Design: Design Alliance, Inc.
Typesetting: the dotted i

Published by Dearborn Trade Publishing
A Kaplan Professional Company

Printed in the United States of America

03 04 05 06 07 10 9 8 7 6 5 4 3 2 1

Library of Congress Cataloging-in-Publication Data

Bernstein, Jacob, 1946-
    No bull investing : straightforward advice to maximize your returns in
any market, with any amount of money / Jake Bernstein.
      p.   cm.
    Includes index.
    ISBN 0-7931-6274-2 (6x9 paperback)
    1. Investments. 2. Finance, Personal. I. Title.
HG4521.B4443 2003
332.6—dc21

2003001186

Dearborn Trade books are available at special quantity discounts to use for sales promotions, employee premiums, or educational purposes. Please call our Special Sales Department to order or for more information, at 800-621-9621, ext. 4404, or e-mail trade@dearborn.com.

CONTENTS

Introduction   vii

PART ONE   PREPARATIONS

1. WANT TO MAKE MORE MONEY? DO THESE THINGS FIRST   1

Who Am I?   4
A Few of the Things I Learned and Why I Want to Share Them with You   9

2. BEGINNINGS, DANGERS, AND DIRECTIONS   19

Of Course You Want to Take Immediate Action!   20
The Dangers of Moving Too Slowly   21
Do It Alone or Get a Partner?   22
A Checklist for Successful Preparation   23

3. MARRIAGE, MONEY, AND FAMILY   33

Investing and Marriage Issues   33
Harnessing the Synergism of a Two-Income Family   34
Life Insurance on Both Partners: Term, Convertible Term, or Other   35
Tax Considerations and Strategies   37
Planning for the Financial Burden of Having Children   38
Protecting Your Assets from Legal Ramifications   40
You and Your Spouse as Investment Partners   42

4. SELF-KNOWLEDGE: Your Practical and Emotional Selves   45

Investor Behavior   46
Mastering the Psychological Aspects of Investing   50
The Majority Is Usually Wrong—Don't Forget That!   53

5. SETTING FINANCIAL GOALS   55

Many Investors Have Been Losers   58
Victims of the System   63

A Few General Rules to Get You Started   64
The "Boring" Part of Setting Financial Goals   73

PART TWO   STRATEGIES AND ALTERNATIVES

6. THE GENERAL INVESTMENT MODEL   81

An Overview of the General Investment Model (GIM)   81
The Setup, Trigger, and Follow-Through Method (STF)   92
The STF in Detail   96
Summary   99

7. THE METHOD   101

Selection and Timing of Investments   102
Introducing the Method   106
Introducing Momentum   109
How to Calculate Momentum   111
What Does Momentum Tell Us about a Market?   112
Divergence and Changes in Trend   113
Timing, Timing, Timing   117
Where Do I Get the MOM?   120
Practice, Practice, Practice!   120

8. GAMBLE OR INVEST YOUR WAY TO WEALTH?   129

The Instant Age   132
Contradictions, Conflicts, and Consistency   132
Narrowing the Field of Choices   133
How the Stock Market Can Be a Gamble   137
How the Stock Market Can Be an Investment   138
How the Stock Market Can Be Used for Trading   138
Real Estate and the General Investment Model   139
The Good News and the Bad News in Futures Trading   140

9. STRATEGIES FOR A SHOESTRING BUDGET   143

The Three Shoestring-Budget Starting Levels   145
$5,000 Available Starting Capital   146
How Dollar Cost Averaging Works   146
Drip Your Way to Success   151
Less Than $2,500 Available Starting Capital   151
A Few Portfolio Suggestions for Beginners and Small Investors   154

10. GETTING SERIOUS: Strategies Beyond the Shoestring Budget   157

From $5,000 to $20,000   157
More Than $10,000 but Less Than $25,000   158
More Than $25,000 but Less Than $50,000   159
More Than $50,000   159
Investing in Precious Metals and Coins   159
Protecting Yourself with Investments in Rare Coins   162
Numismatics and Numismatic Coin Investment Programs   168
Guidelines for Investing in Coins   170
Fast and Furious—The Hottest Games in Town   172

PART THREE   LOOKING AHEAD

11. STAYING AHEAD OF THE CURVE: Emerging Opportunities   177

What's Ahead in the Area of Technological Breakthroughs?   178

12. SUMMARY AND FINAL THOUGHTS   181

A Perspective on Investor Psychology   181
Economic Yin and Yang: Cycles of Boom and Bust   187
Markets Have a Life of Their Own   191
Yesterday, Today, and Tomorrow   192
Summing Up the Lessons Learned   194
Keep in Touch   194

Appendix: Practice Charts and Analyses   195
Online Resources   207
Index   209

INTRODUCTION

Congratulations! I commend you for buying this book. If you have borrowed this book from a library or a friend, then I commend you for being frugal. Saving money is a good thing to do. Perhaps, after you read this book and realize that it offers you many important tips, tools, strategies, and directions for financial success and survival, you may want to buy a copy for yourself and make it a permanent part of your investment resources.

I congratulate you, simply because there are few individuals who are willing to take the time and effort to become financially independent. Most people today are looking for easy answers, easy success, instant success, get-rich-quick schemes, the lottery, and that windfall inheritance from Uncle Louie. The fact that you have taken the time and the trouble to seek out this book—and hopefully to learn from it and use it—sets you apart immediately from the millions who dream of success but who don't have the self-control or discipline to do anything but dream.

The fact that you actively explore your possibilities is a very positive feature of your personality—and therefore I commend you. But what's next? Now that you've decided to read this book, what can you expect? What will this book do for you? Here are some things to consider. If you're in a bookstore as you read these words, then don't even think about buying this book unless you are willing to take the following three steps:

1. *Read and study this book.* Underlining or highlighting the important points that I have made will help you with the next step.

2. *Make a commitment.* Even if it's a small one, commit to put into action one or more of the ideas in this book, *if they appeal to you.* Remember that book learning is one thing, and action is yet another thing. Learning for the sake of learning is fine if you're interested only in academics; however, action is what separates those who succeed from those who only dream of success. And finally . . .

3. *Be consistent.* If you're the kind of person who reads a few pages of a book and then puts the book away, promising to come back to it later, then do yourself a favor and either promise yourself to read this book from cover to cover or put this book down and don't waste your time and money. This book is all about ACTION. If you're PROACTIVE, or want to be, then this is THE BOOK for you. If you're inconsistent, unmotivated, or erroneously believe that success will come to you automatically, forget about this book.

Yes, my opening statements may seem somewhat harsh and direct. But my aim is not to alienate you—not at all. I'm only interested in reaching people who have a burning desire for success. These are the people who will most benefit from this book. And hopefully, their success will prove to be an inspiration to those who presently may be only dreamers.

So, read my book, take my advice seriously, test the waters, and don't let yet another opportunity pass you by. If you do, you'll be old and gray, wondering why you failed to take action when you had so many opportunities. Seize the moment, learn your lessons, and go forward with success!

CHAPTER ONE

WANT TO MAKE MORE MONEY? DO THESE THINGS FIRST

Are you tired of seeing your hard-earned dollars buy you less and less? Are you tired of scrimping and saving to make ends meet? Does your paycheck disappear the minute it goes into the bank? Do you want to make more money? Are you envious of others who ARE making good money in their investments? Are you frustrated because you feel that you don't have the tools to make money? Do you believe that in order to make money as an investor, you will need special skills that can only be acquired in college or through a long course of study? Do you believe that you need a "good broker" in order to make money in the stock market? Do you believe that you need a good real estate broker to make money in real estate? The response to most of these questions is "No." The facts are simple:

- You don't need to be like the millions of people who merely get by, living from paycheck to paycheck.

- You don't need a college degree in finance in order to make money in the stock market; in fact, having such a degree might be detrimental to your success.

- You don't need a good real estate broker in order to make money in the real estate market.

- You don't need to spend hours of research in order to make money in stocks.

- You CAN get the tools you need to become a successful investor.

This book will give you almost everything you need to be a successful investor. All you have to do is to make the commitment and follow through on it. You bought this book in order to make money. So use this book and follow through, or you will have wasted your hard-earned money. Begin on the right footing, be consistent, and you will be more likely to succeed.

This chapter will tear down many of the misconceptions you may have about investing as a way to become financially independent. I will replace any distorted ideas you may have with ones that have not been "polluted" by traditional investment advisors who seek to make you dependent on their advice. You will become your own expert, if you so desire. Will the process be painless? Will success just fall into your lap? Will you merely wake up one morning with newfound wealth? The answer to these questions is "No." However, if you make the effort, you will increase your chances of success, and you will learn skills to serve you well for a lifetime.

The American dream of going from rags to riches has been more than just a dream to hundreds of thousands of people during the 20th century. Today, in spite of the economic slowdown and stock market decline that started in late 1999 and 2000, there are more wealthy people in the United States than ever before. It is a simple fact that our economic system rewards hard work, creativity, motivation, entrepreneurship, self-sufficiency, and ingenuity. In spite of a tax structure that often limits the attainment of wealth and the operation of a successful business, millions of Americans are able to achieve high levels of success.

The doors to success are open to everyone, no matter what their educational level, race, creed, color, or religion may be. While it is sadly true that minorities and women are still discriminated against, it is also true that they have more opportunities for success than ever before. Whether you are a Harvard Law School graduate from a wealthy family or an individual who was raised in the inner city without access to quality education, you can achieve wealth. Although success does indeed depend somewhat on social status, education, political connections, and family wealth, these are not always prerequisites.

Many self-made millionaires have started with virtually no education, no money, no family influence, no political connections, and no assistance. These individuals have made their fortunes based on an idea, on talent, on motivation, on hard work, on persistence, and on the burning desire to rise above their status.

The good news is that there are many ways in which wealth can be achieved in America. The bad news is that the individual who is not blessed with talent to sing or act or play professional sports, or who possesses superb intelligence and a college education in medicine, engineering, law, or science, is often at a distinct disadvantage. There are few vehicles they can use to take them to their goals. This book is about those vehicles. It will help you find the means to achieve your goal of wealth if you are one of the millions who were not blessed with unique skills or talents, family money, or political connections.

Finally, even though there are many avenues for success in a free economy, some methods are more easily implemented than others. Some require less work, and some require less start-up capital. Although I will introduce you to a number of ways in which you can achieve success and financial independence, I will not leave you guessing as to which ones give you the best odds.

WHO AM I?

By now you may be thinking, Who is this guy and why should I listen to him? These are reasonable questions, so let me give you a few reasonable answers. Without going into agonizing detail, suffice it to say that I was raised in a very poor family. I was born in Europe to parents who had been in Nazi concentration camps. My family came to Montreal, Canada, with literally nothing but the clothes on our backs and a few suitcases of personal items. We were taken in by a family who rented us one room in their house. My mother, father, sister, and I shared that one room. My parents worked many hours a day just to pay the rent and put food on the table.

The neighborhood in which I was raised was populated by French Canadian street gangs, ethnic minorities of various types, crime, filth, and failure. My performance in school was pathetic; I barely made passing grades. My father was a piecework tailor working in a clothing factory for many years, and my mother was a seamstress. Getting to and from school each day was like passing through a combat zone. I was often chased and taunted or beaten by gang members. Stealing, fighting, drugs, and other types of crime were rampant. If you were big and strong, mean, and a good fighter, then you were "successful." If you were short and meek, underweight, and undernourished, like I was, then you were a "failure."

Clearly, the law of the jungle ruled on the mean streets of Montreal. Education was frowned on by the gangs and by my peers. School was an evil necessity. The educational system did little to encourage creativity or achievement. School was dull, and the teachers were generally frustrated, underpaid, boring, and punitive. Corporal punishment was condoned, indeed encouraged, and enforced. Minor violations of the rules were often responded to with beatings by the school principal as well as by parents. What was standard procedure then is today considered child abuse.

By law, students who failed to achieve passing grades by the first few terms in high school were sent to vocational schools to learn carpentry, automotive repair, electrical work, construction, or other trades. The system did not reward effort; it merely perpetuated the success of those who were innately intelligent and beat down those who were either unmotivated but intelligent or who were average or below average in intelligence. In short, the system was an abysmal failure.

Understandably, I struggled and suffered, and by age 13, I was told I had no future other than to be a shoemaker or a ditch-digger. The fate of many of my friends would be similar to mine, unless of course they chose crime as a means to achieve success. Some of them did exactly that. Some became street bums, and others died violent deaths at the hands of street gangs. Fortunately, I escaped just in the nick of time.

Through a fortunate twist of fate, my family was given the opportunity to move to the Chicago area. We left the slums and started a new life. My father opened a tailor shop, and my mother, whose skills as a seamstress and dress designer in Canada were only minimally rewarded, did much better in the United States.

Although we were not wealthy by any stretch of the imagination, we did manage to buy a home, a car, and other "creature comforts" that made life more livable. Getting enough food and clothing was no longer an issue for me. And I was no longer afraid of being beaten, tortured, or killed by street gangs. I could walk to school without looking over my shoulder to see if I was about to be attacked. Life was better in many ways, but I quickly discovered the myriad social games that children and adults play in upper-middle-class America.

These games were totally new to me; I knew nothing about the rules of engagement. All I knew was that I was surrounded by wealth and game players, and although the wealth impressed me, the social games sickened me. I had few friends. After all, what person of high class would want to associate with the son of a mere tailor and a seamstress? Still, I managed to make a few friends. In so doing, I discovered that most of the people living in Chicago's northern suburbs had either inherited their money or had made it in the stock market. I discovered that there were opportunities in this country that far surpassed anything I could have achieved in the Montreal ghetto. I learned that even those of average or below-average intelligence had a fighting chance in America. I began to realize that the American dream could be *my* reality.

I watched my parents work 12 to 14 hours a day, seven days a week in order to make ends meet. They supported my sister and me through college and eventually retired to Florida, where they lived out their remaining days before they both died fairly young. By then I was married, had several children, as well as a home, several cars, and many of the things I did not have as a child. I was bound and determined not to follow in my parents' footsteps. Yet, by education I was limited in how much I could earn. In college, I studied clinical psychology. Figuring how much I could earn when I became a full-fledged psychologist, I realized that my potential was limited by the number of patients I could see in one day. Yet, it wasn't a purely moneymaking proposition for me; I had the true and sincere desire to help people.

Not blessed with a wealthy family or a business I could take over from my father or mother, I had to strike out in a new and uncharted direction. Seeking to make my fortune and my mark in an area that was completely different from clinical psychology, I turned to the financial markets because of the limited exposure I had to stock trading in college.

My roommate John at the University of Illinois was an avid stock market investor. Although he was still very young, he had learned the basics of investing and trading from his father, a survivor of the Great Depression and the stock market crash of 1929, as well as many up and down markets since.

John was a very intelligent young man and took to the stock market with all of his energy. He researched stocks, studied market trends, charts, earnings, new products, and stock market behavior. He read the *Wall Street Journal, Barron's Financial Weekly,* the *Wall Street Transcript,* the *Journal of Commerce,* and many other publications that provided in-depth information about the financial markets. In short, he was a true market scholar with a thirst not only for profits but also for the knowledge that could be acquired. He approached the markets as a challenge and sought to solve the deep mystery of market behavior. But there was a problem: he was too young to open a trading account. And that's where I came in.

I was two years older than John, so he convinced me I ought to open an account at the local Hayden-Stone brokerage office in Champaign, Illinois. He offered to fund the account and teach me about the markets, if I made trades for him. As I recall, we also agreed to split the profits, if any, from our venture.

Our first foray into the market was a low-priced Canadian gold mining stock, Wright-Hargreaves, whose ticker symbol at that time was WRT. As I recall, WRT was trading at about $3 per share. We had high hopes for the stock, because it was a gold mining stock and therefore likely to go higher if inflation or political unrest became factors in the U.S. and world economies. Virtually every day, we would venture to the brokerage office to watch the ticker on their large quotation board. We were hypnotized by the tape, watching the numbers change.

We cheered mentally with every price change in WRT: WRT 3 1/16 . . . 3 1/8 . . . 3 3/16. We had visions of great wealth. Of course, WRT didn't make us rich, but the lessons we learned have served us well. From WRT we ventured into other gold mining shares. We studied the South African and Canadian gold companies. We graduated into mobile home stocks, such as Detroit Mobile Home and Fleetwood Enterprises. John was correctly convinced that semiconductor stocks would become big winners in the years ahead.

John encouraged me to read books about the stock market, and I did. To date, the single best book I read was *Reminiscences of a Stock Operator* by Edwin Lefèvre (alias Jesse Livermore). This was one of John's favorite books, and it became one of mine. Today, I own several copies, including one of the original copies from the 1930s. It is a book that I encourage every individual to read, whether he or she is interested in the stock market or not. Why? Because it contains numerous life lessons about human behavior and psychology. These valuable principles are applicable not only to investing but also to business in general and to daily life.

After learning about stocks from John, I ventured off into commodity trading. John and his father were convinced that this would be my ruin. The commodities market was a wild and woolly place in the 1960s, as, to a given extent, it is today. Commodity trading (called futures trading today), was like the Wild West of the investment scene back then. The moves were fast and furious. You could lose all your investment capital in a matter of minutes. But you could make a large amount of money quickly as well, although not as easily.

I was lured into the commodity market by a fast-talking Chicago broker who convinced me to send him $1,000. For those who don't remember economic history, $1,000 in the late 1960s would be the equivalent of $16,000 in the 2000s. A new Volkswagen Beetle cost about $1,600. It wasn't easy for me to part with the money; however, I did so because I was lured by the prospect of making big money. After all, the broker virtually guaranteed me that I could make $18,000 that year, and I was not pleased with my earning prospects in the field of psychology. Because my father was a hardworking tailor who rarely earned more than $5,000 a year in his business, the prospect of earning $18,000 a year or more was very attractive.

My venture, or more correctly my adventure, into the commodity markets was a mixed blessing. At first, I was a winner, and then I was a loser. It's a story all too frequently repeated in the commodity markets. But the good news was that I learned a great deal, not only about trading but also about myself. My experiences led me to do research on market behavior in stocks and commodities as well as in economic trends.

Through my research, I learned a number of valuable concepts that have served me well now for many years. I will share these with you, because I truly believe that these lessons will help you achieve your goal of financial independence, no matter how old you are, which markets or businesses you plan to go into, and what your level of experience may be as an investor.

I believe these concepts as well as their methods of application can be your keys to success, even if you begin with a very small amount of capital. I also believe that these concepts and methods can help anyone achieve the American dream, no matter the level of education, social status, and current profession.

A FEW OF THE THINGS I LEARNED AND WHY I WANT TO SHARE THEM WITH YOU

My experiences have taught me valuable lessons that everyone who wants to achieve financial independence should know and take to heart. Although some of the lessons may not seem especially relevant to you at this time, I assure you they will become important to you when you realize that the good life in a capitalist society is a pure function of money and success. Now I am not, in any way, shape, or form, suggesting that everything revolves around money. Clearly, it does not. Family, friends, spirituality, social awareness and action, as well as ethics and commitment are all part and parcel of a balanced and well-integrated personality. But these are outside the scope of this book. Remember: No matter how much success you may achieve financially, your gains will amount to nothing if you fail to develop other important aspects of your life.

There are several reasons I want to share these things with you. First and foremost, I believe that every individual who lives in a democratic, capitalist society is entitled to share in the progress and wealth that defines such societies. Although we will not all be fabulously wealthy, we are all capable of living very comfortably if we set our minds and actions to success.

Second, and of considerable importance to me, I want to give back to society some of what it has given to me. In other words, I want to offer thousands of individuals, perhaps hundreds of thousands, the opportunity to be successful using the tools that took me many years to accumulate. And third, I want to know that I have made an impact, that I have made my mark on society, and that I have hopefully helped improve the lives of many people.

Not too long ago, I received a complaint by e-mail from a woman who had read a book I coauthored with my son, Elliott Bernstein, titled *Stock Market Strategies That Work* (McGraw-Hill Professional, 2002). She told me there were some errors in the book. I asked her what the errors were and, on receiving her reply, I sent a thorough response to her questions, as well as a detailed response to questions she asked that were not part of the book she had read.

She wrote back, telling me that she was still upset about the errors she found and that she wanted to return the book. Rather than thank me even once for the knowledge the book gave her, she was intent on complaining about the $19.95 she had spent. I replied again, telling her that she ought to return the book if she was so totally dissatisfied, and that I would still be willing to help her with any questions she had *free of charge*. My interest was purely to assist her. I did not, as some individuals in my profession do, tell her that my consultation fee was $500 per hour or that she needed an appointment.

Still, she focused her energies on complaints rather than solutions. She implied that my purpose in writing books was to make money and not to educate. Apparently, she did not understand that writing books like this one generally yields only a small amount of money for the author, and that the book would likely sink into obscurity after a year or two. Let me tell you again that my goals are first and foremost to educate and to have an impact on society, hopefully to improve the lot of average individuals.

My lessons in the stock and commodity markets taught me a number of basic but highly important facts.

Patterns Are the Key to Success in Virtually Any Business or Investment

By this I mean that history repeats itself not only in the markets and in economies but also in business ventures. All things in life follow cyclical patterns. Cycles begin at a low point, rise to a peak, and then decline, only to repeat the process. Think of your own life and experiences in this context. Think about your successes and failures. Think about your relationships. I will elaborate on this highly important fact of life repeatedly throughout this book. For now, take my word that life is full of patterns, and that if we know the patterns—of life, of investing, and of economics—then we have improved our odds of success substantially.

Time Is More Important Than Price

We are all preoccupied with price. We bargain for lower prices, even though we want to buy a given item. Sometimes, we miss the opportunity to buy or sell because we waited for a certain price. Though well-to-do in their own right, my in-laws will travel nine miles to buy grapes for ten cents a pound less than they can buy them locally.

Investors who were bitten by the gold bug in the 1970s believed the Hunt brothers when they predicted gold would rise to $1,000/oz. and silver to $100/oz. They bought at the right time, but today, over 25 years later, they're still waiting for the markets to hit these predicted price targets. Their mistake was that they were thinking in terms of price and not in terms of time. If the time was right to exit gold and silver, then what did it matter if the price was right? Hundreds, if not thousands, of investors thought if United Airlines had declined from over $100 per share in 1997 to $20 per share in 2002, that it was dirt cheap. At $10 per share it was absurdly cheap. At $5 per share it was a steal. At under $3 per share, the company was forced to declare bankruptcy. Price was unimportant—time was the critical factor. Was the time right for investing in United Airlines? Clearly it was not! Those who acted on price alone lost money. Those who refused to buy the stock because the TIME to buy was not right were spared considerable grief and losses.

I learned that if my TIMING is right in starting a business, buying a stock, selling a stock, or staying out of a given business, then the PRICE was right no matter what it was. What may look expensive one day may be seen as very cheap a few days later, *if the timing* of a move is correct. Perhaps the most important lesson you will learn from me is NOT to think in terms of price but rather to think in terms of time and timing. If the time to take a given form of action is right, then the price must be right, no matter what it may be!

Most Investors Lose Most of the Time

It's a simple but powerful fact. It's a sad but true fact. It's a fact of investment life. The odds are that if you don't invest your money with a solid plan, you are likely to lose. The odds are that if you don't start a new business with a solid plan and a firm direction, you will lose. The odds are that if you try to manage your own money without knowledge, you will likely lose. It's that simple, and it's that universal.

To Be Successful You Must Anticipate Things before They Happen

It's called planning, insight, foresight, forward-thinking, and good business. In the stock market, you will need to think ahead and make plans based on your EXPECTATIONS. In business, you will need to do the same. Success in real estate also functions on this simple but powerful rule. Success involves a formula that is based on anticipation of change, preparing for that change, and then moving on to the next opportunity once your expectations have become realities. A specific model for doing this will be presented later on.

Contrary Opinion Is One of the Most Important Tools to Success

The contemporary way of saying this is "Think outside the box." In other words, you will want to go contrary to the crowd most of the time. This won't make you feel too good, and it won't rest well with some of your friends, family, or associates. By "contrary opinion," I mean simply that you must assess the prevailing majority opinion, and you must be willing to think and DO the opposite. When most people are afraid to buy stocks or to begin a certain type of business, then you must seriously consider buying stocks or starting a business.

When most people are convinced that things are good, and that the good times will never end, you must take actions that will serve you well when the good times do end. When most people are panicking, you must be calm and collected, taking logical steps instead of reacting irrationally. When most people are pessimistic, you want to be an optimist. There are literally hundreds of examples in business where contrary opinion paid big dividends. The most recent example was the much-vaunted, much-feared "Y2K bug," which was supposed to bring with it financial chaos, the collapse of the power grid, anarchy, mass confusion, and worse. Some of the most well-known analysts, politicians, and scientists staked their reputations on the belief that cataclysmic events—socially, politically, economically, and technologically—would happen when the new millennium started. And nothing happened.

We were warned by the prophets of gloom and doom that banks might close down, that we might not have electricity, that we might not be able to have medical prescriptions filled, and that food distribution would stop or be curtailed. The Y2K bug was one of the most obvious examples of how panic can be infectious. If you'd like more examples, read *McKay's Extraordinary Popular Delusions and the Madness of Crowds* (Xlibris Corp., 30 November 2000).

I'll make it very simple and straightforward for you: What most people think is wrong and when most people are thinking one way, odds are that events will develop the opposite way. Yes, it will be very difficult for you to be a contrary thinker, but it can yield great rewards.

You Have to Think for Yourself

This seems very obvious, doesn't it? We all want to believe that we think for ourselves. In truth, we are brainwashed daily by the media, by newspapers, and by friends, family, and those we love. Does this mean that you should not read newspapers, watch television, or listen to the radio? Should you also disrespect those you love? Not at all! The answer is simple: Develop your ideas independently, evaluating all other ideas and statements within the framework of what you believe yourself. It's easy to be influenced by other people, especially if you love and respect them.

The sophisticated, intelligent-looking, smooth-talking anchorperson on business television or the nightly news may appear to know what he or she is talking about. The odds are that they know nothing more than what they're reading. Their script has been prepared for them; they're merely reading the words that other people have written for them. Who are these other people? Do they have hidden agendas? Do they know what they're talking about? Are they merely reflecting the opinions of others? You'll find that most of the time their thinking is very standard, very average, and very wrong. So, remember to think for yourself!

The More Complicated Your Methodology, the Less Likely It Is to Work

During my more than 30 years in the investment field, I have seen literally hundreds, if not thousands, of trading strategies, investment schemes, programs, multilevel marketing programs, Internet sales programs, computer trading programs, real estate methods, and more. Most of them don't work. And the ones that are the most complicated seem to be the least successful. Although it has likely been grossly overused, the "Keep It Simple, Stupid," or KISS, rule is still one of the best rules you can learn. You don't need a degree in economics or business to make money as an investor. All you need is a plan, some rules, motivation, some money, discipline, and consistency.

These, then, are the universal truths I discovered during my lengthy search for methods that would make me financially independent. I will elaborate on them throughout the course of this book. Rest assured that if you learn them and apply them to any business, investment plan, or trading program, they will serve you well. Ignore them, and you will be destined to learn the same lessons over and over until you finally get them right!

Many Roads Lead to Success

This book is not just about the stock market; it will give you a general formula for making money in any market, whether real estate, rare coins, options, futures, single stock futures, bonds, mutual funds, or other moneymaking ventures. The way I will achieve this goal is by providing you with concepts, structure, examples, and a general model you can follow. The model will serve you well as long as you use it. It will not serve you, if you try to sidestep it or change it. I will also give you specific examples of how to put your plan for financial freedom into action.

As we move forward and explore the various avenues and methods by which you can achieve your goals and realize your dreams, know that the journey ahead will not be an easy one. Success will not "fall out of a magazine." It will take work and effort, but vast rewards await you. In fact, you may even enjoy the challenge. Remember that attaining and maintaining success require a diversified approach. Keep the big picture in mind as you specialize in one area or in one type of investment, because there are other aspects of investing and financial planning that will need your attention as well. All too often, individuals focus on a single aspect of investing and make good money, but fail to plan ahead. The result is that they lose money either to taxes and inflation or in other investments they should not have ventured into without full information and knowledge. In short, you have to learn how to make money, how to keep it, how to make it grow, how to protect it, and how to spend it wisely.

CHAPTER TWO

BEGINNINGS, DANGERS, AND DIRECTIONS

No matter how you look at it, investing always involves some degree of risk or danger. You can't get ahead unless you're willing to take some risk. There are many forms of risk, however. You can risk your money or your time. You can risk your physical and mental health. You can risk your relationships. Although many people may believe that the only risk in investing is money, I can tell you from many years of experience that they are wrong. Investing carries many risks. These risks increase as a function of who you are, how you invest, how you view your investments, and how you handle your life in general. It is not possible to separate the investment from the investor. Two investors can have the same ideas about the same investments, and they can achieve distinctly different results depending on how they put their plans into action. Two people looking at the same information will *not* necessarily reach the same conclusions. That's why there are buyers and sellers in any market. A piece of property that may seem expensive to one person may be an amazing bargain to another. Where opportunities abound for some people, only risk of loss exists for others.

The first thing you must know about making your money grow and becoming financially independent is that there is and will always be some degree of risk. Yes, you *can* lose money. But what will it cost you to *not* take some risk? Will stress force you to take losses in another way? Are you willing to accept the physical stress of working several jobs and long hours to make ends meet? Are you willing to accept the stress that long hours will exact on your family relationships? Are you willing to accept the emotional stress, anxiety, and pressure that occur when you can't pay the rent on time? All of these are forms of losses. You can either accept these losses, or you can take the risk of a financial loss as a means of avoiding other types of losses. The decision is yours. Either you take one type of risk to avoid another, or you accept the losses that may occur as a result of having insufficient money to support yourself and your family.

OF COURSE YOU WANT TO TAKE IMMEDIATE ACTION!

Perhaps I struck a chord in your thinking, and you spent some time considering your situation. After consideration, have you decided that there is some merit to my view? Have you decided that you want to become financially independent? Maybe I convinced you that you can indeed do it yourself, that you don't need an education in finance or a broker to advise you. In short, are you willing to take the chance?

If you have decided to take action, then stop for a moment and think. Some people want to act immediately; in fact, they want to act too quickly. Learning how to make your money grow is not like learning to play a game of Monopoly. Learning how to make your money grow cannot be achieved by sitting in a one-hour class or seminar on investing. It's not as simple as following the advice in a newsletter or taking a stock tip from a friend or relative. But it is not nearly as complicated as you might think. One thing you will need to remember: Take your time. Don't rush into investing simply because you feel financial pressure. I have observed that many people do more research when buying a television than they do making an investment. Moving too quickly can cause mistakes, and investment mistakes will cost you money.

THE DANGERS OF MOVING TOO SLOWLY

There is also danger in taking too much time. After all, book learning can only take you so far; you'll have to get your feet wet sooner or later. Sooner or later you will have to invest some real money, even if it's only a few hundred dollars. You will have to put your knowledge to work eventually. Unfortunately, many would-be investors freeze up when it comes time to make the fateful decision. They believe that they need more information, that they have not learned enough. They hide behind their feelings of ignorance in order to avoid taking the leap. The fact is that they are afraid to lose money, and they believe the best way to avoid losing money is to be absolutely certain of their decision. Although it's a good idea to take your time, it's a bad idea to take too much time. Don't rush into an investment, but don't become an eternal student, either.

DO IT ALONE OR GET A PARTNER?

Now you must make yet another decision before you begin to invest your money. You must decide whether you will learn the business of investing on your own or with a partner. There are good points and bad points about each of these avenues. I will examine these more fully in Chapter 9, but for now consider these points:

- Working with a partner allows you to share in your enthusiasm.

- A partner can help you remain motivated.

- Working with a partner can be beneficial, because you can pool your financial resources.

- Your decisions can be double-checked if you have a partner.

- A partner can provide meaningful input about things you may not have seen.

- A partner can help you maintain discipline.

On the other hand, there can be a downside to working with a partner. Consider these potential limitations of working with a partner:

- You may have a personality conflict or clash with a partner.

- Your own good judgment could be adversely affected by working with a partner.

- You may end up quarreling with your partner about profits and/or losses.

- Sometimes, opinions can become infectious, particularly if your partner is highly persuasive. If his or her ideas or analyses of the facts are wrong, you may get fooled into going along with him or her and lose money as well.

Your partner need not be a business associate or a friend. You can embark on your investment plan with a spouse or even a close friend. Remember, however, that sometimes being too involved with your partner outside your investment relationship can lead to problems. Some of these are discussed in Chapter 3.

A CHECKLIST FOR SUCCESSFUL PREPARATION

I have spent considerable time in this chapter discussing the importance of effective and thorough preparation. I have given you some ideas about directions to take, as well as which assets and possible liabilities of the numerous alternatives are available to you as an investor. Here is a ten-item checklist that may help you in the planning stages. I suggest that you consider these points carefully within the framework of who you are and what you want to accomplish as an investor.

1. Are You Willing to Make the Commitment?

This is the single most important point on my list. If you can't make the commitment to begin your plan and, most important, to stay with it for at least several years, then you may as well take your money and gamble with it. Odds are that you won't be successful as an investor other than by pure luck. You will need to make money the "good old-fashioned way." You'll have to earn it. The good news is threefold: if you make the commitment and keep it, you won't have to work hard, the work will be enjoyable, and your odds of success will be significant.

2. Is the Money You Plan to Invest Risk Capital or Vital to Your Financial Survival?

You can't succeed if you're playing with "scared money"; that is, money you are afraid to lose or may need to make a car payment or pay the rent. Although your goal as an investor is to make your money grow as strongly and as quickly as possible, there will always be the risk of loss. Unless you can accept this fact, your probability of success will be low indeed. Simply stated: The money you have allocated to investing is not to be used for any other purpose, until you have achieved a reasonable degree of success. If you can't afford to play the game, you owe it to yourself to avoid becoming involved in the venture! Even if you can only afford $25 per month, you *can* become an investor. Your progress will be slower than if you start with more money, but the important thing is just to begin.

3. Determine Where You Stand in Terms of Your Individual Needs and Goals

The right investments for a retired automobile worker may not be the right investments for a 35-year-old surgeon. The right investments for a college student who has a part-time job may not be the right investments for a middle-aged housewife who runs a small business part-time out of her home. The right investments for someone who earns over $500,000 per year may not be the right investments for an individual whose income is in the $100,000-per-year range. Because everyone has different experiences, risk tolerance, available investment capital, family situations, tax considerations, obligations, and temperaments, what constitutes an appropriate investment plan will vary considerably from one individual to the next. No one book, course, or seminar can give you everything you need. However, if you study the general models and techniques presented here, you will likely fare well no matter what specific investments you make within the limits and needs of your situation. Knowing where you stand, what you need, and how you plan to get there is of primary importance. This book provides numerous suggestions and directions for accomplishing this goal.

4. Do You Have the Time to Follow Through on Your Commitment?

People are so busy these days. They rush to work and rush home. They run to catch the train, eat lunch quickly—often at their desk while working—and rush from the office or the assembly line to the gym. They hurry to the supermarket and then home to throw something together for dinner. They carpool for the kids and take them to after-school activities, overnights with their friends, Boy Scouts, Girl Scouts, school choir, karate, and even Sunday school. We argue—rightfully—that we need more time to enjoy life, to enjoy the fruits of our labors, to go fishing or skiing, or to take a long cruise. When we add having to spend time investing our money, it just doesn't seem fair or right. After all, we work so hard to get ahead. We give so much to our children and our jobs and families.

Why should we have to add yet another significant responsibility to our list of chores? The simple answer to this reasonable and perennial question is: There *is* time, and everyone can afford to set aside several hours a week to plan for his or her future. Time must be budgeted, and priorities need to be established. I am a firm believer in the fact that children, as much as we may love them, cannot take all of our time. I have seen too many people give too much and then become bitter about not having enough time for themselves. I have been guilty of doing so my-self. Remember that without proper planning and investing, you may be limiting the ability of your children to attend the college or professional school of their choice. When you plan and implement your investments, you're doing so not only for your retirement but also for your children's future.

If you are single and don't have children, then you may need to cut back a bit on your social life if you want to ensure a finan-cially secure future for yourself. No matter what your situation or position in life, you *can* find the time to plan your invest-ments. As in the case of having sufficient investment capital, having the time can be adjusted to your needs. You say you don't have two hours a week—no problem. How about one hour a week? Or 30 minutes? If you can't spend a few hours a week, then go more slowly and spend 30 minutes a week. If you can't find 15 minutes a week to do your homework on investing, then don't even bother reading the rest of this book. That's the real-ity of the situation!

5. Be Consistent, Organized, and Thorough in All You Do

Perhaps you are a disorganized person, as I am. Perhaps your desk is piled high with papers, notes, books, and mail. Maybe you have not mastered the skills of organization and follow-through. If you believe, as I do, that disorganization will limit or even prevent you from being successful, then you will have the incentive to make changes. Note that I am not suggesting a com-plete change in your life. You can continue to be a disorganized, messy person in all else you do, but when it comes to investing, you will need to change. And you'll need to change sooner rather than later.

If there is any one aspect of investing that can be facilitated with the assistance of a partner, it is the area of organization. If you don't have what it takes to be consistent and organized, then I urge you to find a partner who possesses these skills. As you continue to read this book and become more experienced as an investor, you will appreciate more fully the benefits of being organized. If you decide to work with a partner, then make certain that you choose your partner carefully and with forethought. Don't be afraid to interview potential partners and set specific ground rules before you get started, in order to make certain that he or she possesses the skills that will complement yours.

6. Out with the Old and in with the New

To a given extent, most of us are victims of the traditional approach to investing. In other words, we have been indoctrinated to view investing in a particular way. The usual approach to investing is perpetuated by economics courses in high school and college, by popular books, and by financial advisors and stockbrokers. We have been told that we need to follow the time-tested principles of investing. Many of these principles are—in my view—outdated ideas are no longer applicable or effective in today's investment environment. For example, investors have been brainwashed to believe that in order to make money in stocks, they need to know what a company does.

You need to know the market for its products, its management, its financial history and stability, its earnings, its projected earnings, and much more. You need to know the economic outlook, the probable direction of interest rates, the potential effect of domestic and international politics, the degree of professional buying or selling in the stocks you want to buy, and much more. In short, we have been led to believe that the only

way to make money in stocks—or for that matter, in real estate—
is by becoming a financial expert.

This myth has, I believe, been perpetuated by a financial community that seeks to make investors dependent on the advice of
their brokers. Whether in the real estate market, stocks, mutual
funds, futures, or options, we have been led to believe that we
need a good broker in order to make money. I suggest that this
is a false assumption and that, in fact, depending on a broker for
advice can, in many cases, lead you to losses rather than profits.

The fact is that there are very few brokers in any field whose
selections and recommendations have a lengthy and profitable
track record. And these individuals are so good at what they do
that they accept only the largest clients who can make their efforts worthwhile financially. In fact, some of the most successful
investors do not depend on brokers for advice. They have become their own experts. Before you accept the traditional ideas,
ask yourself the following questions:

- Why do so many people still lose money following the advice
  of brokers who are touted as being "good" at what they do?

- Why do mutual funds that are managed by individual experts or teams of experts still decline in value when the
  stock market goes down? Isn't it fair to ask why these experts
  cannot minimize declines and still beat the overall market?

- Why have so many "top" analysts lost their jobs or fallen
  into disrepute for taking money to recommend stocks
  that they knew were likely to go bankrupt?

- Why have various agencies of the U.S. government fined
  major brokerage houses for having a conflict of interest
  wherein they recommended worthless stocks in order to
  sell them to unsuspecting investors?

These are only some of the limitations to consider about the traditional view and methods of investing. The methods you will learn in this book will help you become an independent investor, which will help you avoid dependence on brokers, analysts, and advisors.

7. Be Prepared to Play Your Own Game

All too often your plans to become an independent investor and increase your wealth will be thwarted by those around you. I am speaking specifically of family and "friends." People tend to get jealous, even over the smallest things. The fact that you are forging ahead, taking charge, and controlling your financial future will cause some of your friends and family to be envious. They may try to discourage you from investing. They may attempt to dissuade you by saying that your efforts will amount to nothing but losses. Don't listen to them! In fact, I urge you to make your investment plans without telling friends or family (other than your spouse), because odds are that few people will be supportive. It is best to play your own game and decide what types of investing *you* want to do. Gather the knowledge you will need and then begin your venture (adventure) without announcing, discussing, or asking permission of friends or family.

8. Don't Fool Yourself into Thinking You Need Expensive Computers or Programs

If you allow yourself to believe that an expensive computer and the latest programs are needed in order to succeed as an investor, then you are dead wrong! Here is yet another example of how the average investor has been tricked into believing what the professional community wants to sell to investors. The simple facts are as follows:

- A considerable amount of quality investment information is available via the Internet *free of charge*. Yes, you will need a computer to access the Internet information, but you can do that with the most basic of computers or an Internet café.

- An expensive computer, or for that matter, any type of computer, will not necessarily help you make money if you cannot use it properly, and if you don't have the right programs. Even if you do have the right computer and the right programs, there is no guarantee you will do better than if you did all of your work manually without trading or investing software.

- You don't need a broker to get stock prices. You don't need a broker in order to find real estate. And you don't even need a broker to invest in stock programs called dividend reinvestment programs, or DRIPs. You can buy shares in a company directly from the company itself, bypassing the broker entirely without paying a penny in brokerage commissions.

9. Don't Feel Pressured at Any Time, for Any Reason

If you allow yourself to be pressured into buying or selling stocks, options, futures, real estate, coins, or any other type of investment, then you are likely making the wrong decision. You need to act slowly, diligently with focus and with purpose. If you feel a significant urgency to make an investment, then you are likely being influenced by someone else, either a friend or a broker, or by something you have heard on the radio, read in the newspaper, or seen on television. There are thousands of stocks, millions of properties, and tens of thousands of business opportunities, none of which will work for you if you don't take the time to study, analyze, and act. Such decisions cannot be made quickly until you have experience and understanding. If you feel pressure to invest, even after reading this book, then you are likely headed for disaster. My warning holds true for any investment, at any time, even after you have had significant experience.

10. Be Prepared to Diversify

Although you can seek to become an expert in one very narrow area of investing, you are better off if you seek to diversify your knowledge and investments into several different areas. Putting all your eggs into one basket will serve you well as long as that one area is performing well. However, if this one area begins to falter, then you will be left out in the cold without a fall-back position. Diversification of investments and assets will be discussed in Chapters 5, 9, and 10.

CHAPTER THREE

MARRIAGE, MONEY, AND FAMILY

By now, you're hopefully chomping at the bit to learn some of the investment techniques to which I alluded in Chapters 1 and 2. I ask you to be patient, so that we can take care of first things first. If you're a single person, you can skip this chapter for now, unless you have imminent marriage plans. If you're married, then I suggest you read this chapter before you begin your investment plans or, at the very minimum, make your investment plans with this chapter in mind.

INVESTING AND MARRIAGE ISSUES

Can marriage hurt or help your financial situation? This chapter will give you some straight talk about the pitfalls of poor planning and preparation prior to marriage, as well as some details on how to improve your finances once you're married. This chapter will tell you how to approach the financial and legal sides of marriage from a practical and profit-oriented perspective. If you fail to adequately prepare yourself for the challenges and opportunities that marriage can provide, you may well fall victim to its limitations on your success. The power of a two-income family can be harnessed to produce very large financial gains, or it can be a drag on your path to success and wealth as well as early retirement. There are actions you must take either before you make those wedding vows or shortly afterward. If you're already married, then fear not—it's not too late!

HARNESSING THE SYNERGISM OF A TWO-INCOME FAMILY

There is no doubt that the two-income family clearly is an advantage, if you learn to use it properly when you make your investments. I strongly suggest you consider one of the incomes for purposes of paying bills, rent, food, and other expenses, and the other income for investing. Naturally, if the two incomes are necessary in order to take care of bills and living expenses, then consider a portion of the second income for investment purposes. As a rule of thumb, I would suggest approximately 25 percent as a minimum for investing. Realistically, this may not be possible for you. If not, you will need to begin on a much smaller scale. See Chapter 9 for details. Clearly, the more you can invest from a second income, the faster you will be able to achieve financial independence. Naturally, if you are a "DINK" (dual income no kids), you will have more investment capital. I cannot stress too strongly the importance of beginning your investment program before you get married and no later than the first year of your marriage, when you may have two incomes and no children. You may even want to consider delaying parenthood until you have built a solid investment foundation with the assistance of a dual income.

LIFE INSURANCE ON BOTH PARTNERS:
Term, Convertible Term, or Other

The issue of life insurance is a touchy but necessary one. There are those who claim that life insurance is not necessary if you're a good investor. Of course, there are arguments both in favor of and opposed to this view. There are a number of different types of insurance that cover the spectrum from investment-grade insurance, or whole life insurance, to term insurance on the other extreme. The investment type of whole life insurance works on a simple concept. You pay premiums either monthly or quarterly, and if you die your spouse collects, or vice versa. The amount of the premium is a function of your age, health, and the size of the policy you buy. There are various formulas by which you can compute how much insurance you need based on your earning power and the financial needs of your family.

Any competent insurance agent can help you with this. He or she will gladly show you alternatives based on projections. Generally speaking, these projections are honest and reasonable based on the information you have given the agent about yourself and your family. The amount you pay for coverage—the premium—can vary considerably, so be sure to shop around. There are many Web sites that can assist you in finding the right insurance at the lowest price. Remember that with this type of insurance, you want to be as confident as possible that the company you are insured with will not go broke. In order to determine this, you may have to do some research. The cheapest may not be the best! The good news about this type of policy is that the money you pay in is an investment.

At some time in the future, you will be able to collect what you paid in, and you may be able to borrow against it. But don't expect your investment to grow substantially, because insurance companies invest very conservatively, and the return will be low. While life insurance is usually a safe investment, it won't make you rich and won't grow quickly. The good news is that you and your family will be protected. The key issue with this type of investment is whether you can make your money grow faster than the insurance company can, and whether you can still get the coverage you need.

This is where term insurance comes into play. With term insurance, your premiums are much lower than they are with whole life insurance, but you don't get anything back. The money goes down the drain, unless the insured person dies. There are some tremendous bargains in term insurance. For most individuals, this is the sensible way to go because the cost is low and the protection is good. But term insurance will only be to your benefit if you can take the money you saved by not buying whole life insurance and invest it wisely. And that's a big "if."

Which Is Right for You?

Although you are not locked into one type of insurance or another, as you learn how to invest your money (which is the purpose of this book), you will only need term insurance. And this is what I recommend. Note also that there are other plans that fall somewhere between term insurance and whole life. Insurance companies offer a wide range of alternatives. Here are some pointers that will, I believe, serve you well, if you have the financial ability to put them into action:

- Take term insurance for yourself and your spouse.

- Don't go overboard on the amount of coverage. As long as costs remain low and within your ability to pay, buy the largest amount you can reasonably afford.

- Buy the same amount of coverage for yourself and your spouse to avoid any potential conflict due to problems of ego. I have seen many conflicts arise between husband and wife about the size of a policy. If the husband feels that he should have $1 million in insurance but wants only $500,000 insurance on his wife, his wife may feel belittled. Avoid any problems and just consider that husband and wife are equally important.

- Buy whole life insurance for your children. This form of investment is all too often overlooked. The cost of buying such insurance for young and healthy children can be very low. If you begin with whole life for children when they are very young, you can buy a good amount of coverage, and by the time your children are ready for college, they could have a good little next egg put away.

- Upgrade your insurance coverage as your income increases. This suggestion speaks for itself and requires no elaboration.

- If you have whole life insurance now, phase it out and switch to term insurance as you become a more successful investor.

TAX CONSIDERATIONS AND STRATEGIES

As you may know, married couples who file a joint return have been effectively penalized on their taxes for many years. This archaic part of the tax code is likely to fall by the wayside in the next few years. In the past, however, some couples have opted to file separately or, in extreme cases, to avoid marriage in order to avoid the penalty. This is not necessary if you are investing successfully. In addition, deductions for dependents can be a great help. If you have a unique situation with regard to dependents, you are advised to consult your tax advisor for information and strategies.

PLANNING FOR THE FINANCIAL BURDEN OF HAVING CHILDREN

I have already given you my suggestions for whole life insurance for children. But there are other things you can do for your children, and you *must* do them when the children are very young. First and foremost among these are the following:

- Establish a mutual fund account for each child. You will get more details about this in Chapters 8, 9, and 10.

- Educate your children in money and its meaning as soon as possible.

- Promote the value and history of being an investor by "indoctrinating" your children as soon as they are capable of understanding. Some of you may think this suggestion is cold, calculating, and mercenary, but the alternative is raising children who do not appreciate the value of money.

- Educate your children in investment techniques when they are very young. There are many games that can assist you, including the traditional Monopoly and Risk games. These games will go a long way to promoting an interest in investing.

- Encourage your children to take an active role in their investments and have them open stock trading accounts as soon as they are legally permitted to do so.

- Educate your children in the dangers of gambling as opposed to the benefits of investing.

- Encourage your children to take investment courses either at school or online.

- Add to your children's motivation by showing them how their investments have grown, and even by allowing them to spend small amounts of their earnings.

How to Lessen the Impact of Paying for College and/or Private Schools

I previously advised you that whole life insurance and mutual funds can be very helpful in planning for college. A number of states have enacted investment plans designed, supposedly, to allow prepayment of tuition in order to defray the cost of rising tuition in the future. Some of these plans are in danger of going broke, and they may not be able to pay off when the time comes. I advise *against* such plans, because they will likely be mismanaged and are too risky. You are better off investing money for college on your own, but this will clearly take discipline, and that's the downside for many people.

Another suggestion is to apply for financial aid even if you have a good income. Most colleges and private schools have substantial endowments and can provide some money toward tuition. This is especially true of private elementary and secondary schools. While some people may feel it is greedy for you to apply for aid if your income is good, the fact is that it's up to the institution to make the decision as to whether you are worthy of assistance or not. It's their decision. If they decide that you can have some money, then take it. And don't feel that you're keeping someone else who is "more needy" than you from having the money. Institutions make their decisions based on the availability of capital and need, but don't hesitate to apply unless your income is very substantial.

PROTECTING YOUR ASSETS FROM LEGAL RAMIFICATIONS

There are many things you can do to protect your hard-earned income from legal attack. All too often, a small mistake can cost you a great deal of money. Yes, you may have insurance to protect you, and you may see yourself as a very cautious person, but in our litigious society no one is immune from attack or frivolous lawsuits. This is why I recommend you make yourself "judgment proof." There are a number of avenues you can take in order to achieve the goal of protecting your assets from legal encumbrances. The primary form of protection is through an entity called a trust. A *trust* is a vehicle that is used to shield your assets from those who would seek to take them in the event of a court ruling against you. Clearly, if your assets are protected, they cannot be taken away. There are various types of trusts that provide different levels of protection. Here are a few types of trusts you may want to consider:

- *Simple trust.* This is a legal arrangement in which an individual (the trustor) gives control of property or money to a person or institution (the trustee) for the benefit of beneficiaries (the people who will eventually benefit from the property or money).

- *Blind trust.* This is a trust in which the beneficiaries do not know what is in the trust and in which an appointed and financially reliable third party has complete management discretion.

- *Pure trust.* BEWARE! If you are actively searching for trusts to protect your assets, you may run into this type of trust. Although its promoters claim that such trusts will protect you from virtually any type of financial assault, their value has not been proven and, in many cases, they have been ruled illegal. Investigate thoroughly before you pay anyone to set up a trust for you, particularly a pure trust. Pure trusts masquerade by many other names, such as common-law trusts, freedom trusts, and so on.

- *Offshore trust.* This is a trust that is set up in a foreign country. By having your assets in a foreign country and a foreign bank, the courts in your country may not be able to seize your money even if there is a judgment against you. Although there are many good things about such trusts, you must be aware of potential legal limitations and tax considerations beforehand. Consult with your attorney and/or tax advisor before you set up a foreign trust.

- *Revocable trust/Living trust.* A revocable trust is often referred to as a living trust. The purpose for establishing a revocable trust is to avoid the time and expense of probate (legal challenges and taxes to your estate in the event of your death or inability to function) and to provide a mechanism for your family members (or other trusted individuals you designate) to take control of your assets should you become incapacitated.

Some individuals and organizations may attempt to convince you that an offshore trust can be a legal way for you to avoid paying taxes. Before you venture into this very gray area, you may want to consult with a tax advisor and/or tax attorney. You may also want to go to the Internal Revenue Service Web site, using the following link: www.ustreas.gov/irs/ci/tax_fraud/2105.pdf. There are numerous books and other Web sites designed to give you expert advice in these areas. I suggest that you consult them. See the Resources at the back of the book for a listing in this area.

YOU AND YOUR SPOUSE AS INVESTMENT PARTNERS

Much has been said in recent years about men "wearing the pants" in the family and the supposed benefits of having the husband manage family investments. I believe that these days are gone forever. My reasoning is based on a number of facts and observations. Generally speaking, I believe that women make better investors than men. Women tend to be less emotional and more logical than men, particularly when it comes to "pulling the trigger," or actually making the investments.

In addition, women tend to be more logical and unemotional when taking losses. They are more likely than men to exit a losing investment. Men tend to make losses a matter of ego as opposed to a matter of fact. Freudian psychologists would have us believe that for a man, taking a loss is like being castrated. Although I won't go that far in the analogy, suffice it to say that most men loathe taking losses. And that often becomes a big problem, because they tend to hang on to losing positions.

Perhaps more important than any of the reasons cited above, investing with a partner adds a good sense of balance to your work. A partner can spot mistakes that you may not see. And a partner can provide another point of view that may prevent losing investments.

Although the democratic process that comes with having a partner can slow things down, in the long run you will likely make better decisions. In the event that your spouse does not want to be included in the process, then you have no choice; however, the opportunity should always be offered to avoid problems later on and to have a more effective overall approach.

In addition, the growing trend toward same-sex marriages and cohabitation in heterosexual relationships without marriage makes inclusion of your partner even more important. I believe that the family that invests together will form stronger bonds and work more effectively toward common goals.

As your children grow older, and if you have given them the opportunity to participate in investment decisions, they will be able to assist you in investment research. Your workload as parents will decrease, and you will also know that you have given your children a head start in the world of capitalism. If by the time your children are in their early teens they are educated in the various aspects of investing, they will be way ahead of their peers. They will see opportunities that others do not see. And you, in turn, will have peace of mind, knowing that your children have a solid financial future ahead of them.

CHAPTER FOUR

SELF-KNOWLEDGE
Your Practical and Emotional Selves

None of the strategies, techniques, or suggestions in this book will be of any use to you unless you have taken the necessary steps to develop your self-discipline and personal psychology. This is by far the weakest link in the chain. Intelligence, achievement in school, and socioeconomic status have very little to do with your psychological skills as an investor. Some of the most intelligent and well-educated individuals are failures as investors. Why? Because they have never been taught the skills that foster and facilitate investment success. This chapter will tell you exactly what you need to do to graduate to the success zone and stay in it.

In this chapter, I will touch on what is one of the most critical issues in successful investing. There are many issues to consider and, depending on your nature and behavior habits, some may be more helpful to you than others. I suggest you read them all and consider them carefully in light of your self-understanding.

INVESTOR BEHAVIOR

Investors are a strange lot indeed. When I made my first futures trade in the summer of 1968, I had no idea that there were as many different approaches to the markets as there were investors and traders. I've also discovered that even though investors say they want to make money in the markets, their behavior often is just the opposite.

I've distilled some of my more important observations of investor behavior into a few pages. I hope you enjoy them, but most of all, I hope you benefit from them. Here, then, in no particular order are my thoughts.

Investors are often too willing to take tips that have no history behind them, while they ignore solid trades with a long history of reliability. Investors often work hard to gather reliable information. They plan their investments, are methodical in setting a risk point, and have the discipline to follow their own research. Yet, all it takes is one urgent call from a broker or one piece of dramatic news, and all their good intentions vanish. They melt into a pool of emotion, abandoning their discipline as they give way to fear and greed.

Investors all too often react impulsively to news, not knowing the odds of success, the risk involved, or the history behind the strategy they have planned. They lose money on the investment opportunity that they took impulsively, and yet they fail to learn from the experience. It seems that the human mind is always looking for an "easy shot." When something comes along that seems easy, discipline appears to deteriorate in spite of all intelligent reasons and past experience to maintain it.

Investors tend to be a very insecure group of individuals when it comes to the implementation of their strategies. What is it that causes investors to commit blunders? Is it lack of knowledge, lack of capital, or lack of a systematic approach? Yes, it can be one or all of these. What it all adds up to is this: Investors tend to wallow in insecurity, no matter how good their research may be. Only the exceptional investor is totally immune to the errors that result from insecurity. Having a solid investment approach, combined with a disciplined approach to implementation, can go a long way toward eliminating most investor insecurity.

Investors love forecasts. Forecasts tend to polarize a person's thinking. They tend to restrict possibilities and give investors tunnel vision. They create a mind-set that is not easily overcome.

Investors poorly execute buy and sell orders in stocks. Investors frequently complain about their price fills. Although there is certainly an element of truth to the complaints, there is also the fact that the overwhelming majority of investors have no idea about how to place orders effectively, or which orders are most suited to their purpose. By merely using the right order at the right time, an investor can save thousands of dollars.

Investors don't like "insiders." An *insider* is an individual who, by virtue of his or her position in a company or otherwise, has knowledge about a pending development in the markets that may not yet be known to the general public. Because investors believe that such knowledge gives insiders an unfair advantage, they are universal in their dislike and mistrust of them. They accuse them of virtually everything from stealing money to fixing prices. Insiders are just as fallible and human as are all investors. The only difference is that they have more experience and know how to "milk" markets for the results they desire. Unfortunately, some of the investment scandals of the early 2000s have helped reinforce public suspicion and mistrust of insiders. Although it may very well be true that those trading with inside information are playing the game unfairly, it is also true that they are not directly responsible for individual investor losses. Ultimately, each investor must evaluate a situation and then take action. Insiders do not force investors to buy or sell stocks or real estate.

Investors hate buying when prices are rising and selling when prices are declining. A costly lesson I've learned from over 30 years in the futures business is the value of buying on strength and selling on weakness. By this I mean that when prices have started an upward trend, the path of least resistance is to buy when prices decline. And when prices are declining, the path of least resistance is to sell when prices go up. Investing with the trend is the most reliable way of making money, whether in stocks, futures, real estate, or collectibles. In spite of the fact that investing with the trend is the more reliable way to make money, many investors shy away from this effective strategy, because they're always afraid of buying too high or selling too low. The average investor is always trying to find a "deal." Although this may work with a street vendor in a flea market, it's not a winning strategy in the financial markets. Many of us have been told that we need to "buy low and sell high" in order to make money. The fact is that we can make money if we "buy high and sell higher." To put it simply, you can board a train that is unlikely to leave the station because it's not in service; you can board a train that's heading back into the garage for repair; or you can board a train whose engine is running as it readies to leave the station. Clearly, the best choice is the train that is ready to leave the station or, better yet, the train that is just pulling out of the station.

Investors hate taking losses—even small ones. This is no surprise to you, is it? This is by far one of the *worst* traits of investors. All too often those little losses, which were not taken when they should have been, turn into account-devouring monsters that can make equity disappear in a matter of days. Many investors would rather allow a small loss of several hundred dollars to turn into a monster than admit to the small loss at the right time.

Investors love to blame everyone but themselves for their losses. Consider the many times you blamed your broker or the insiders for your losses. Most often, we tend to blame everyone but ourselves for losses, but the ultimate responsibility for our investments is our own.

Investors think too much and take too little action. Thinking is good in many aspects of life, even in investing; however, once you have determined your course of action based on your investment approach, you need to take action. All too often, investors fall victim to an affliction called "analysis paralysis." This mental condition expresses itself as the inability to take action due to an oversupply of information. Some investors allow themselves to become bogged down (i.e., paralyzed) by such a large amount of information that they cannot make a decision. This at times serves their purposes, as they avoid the possibility of losing money by not making a decision. Don't think too much. This is not rocket science. Determine your course of action and then make your move.

Investors are inconsistent. At times an investor engages in a behavior or behaviors that are clearly in violation of effective investing rules. Yet, in spite of the fact that rules have been broken, the investment results in a profit. This teaches the investor that consistent following of the rules is not necessary. But because the results of inconsistent rule breaking are random, the investor will never know for certain whether breaking the rules will work or not. The inconsistency of results teaches the investor to react inconsistently.

Investors can't accept too many consecutive losses before they begin to doubt themselves as well as their investment methods. The logic and experience of system testing tells us that some of the best investment methods are subject to considerable draw-downs as well as strings of losing investments. From my experience, I'd have to say that taking as many as seven losses (even up to ten losses) in a row is not unusual. Yet, this is precisely what causes investors to abandon their method or to change midstream. In order to make a method work for you, you have to give it time and plenty of room. Most investors know this intuitively rather than discursively.

Here is how you may embark or stay firmly on the road to consistent profits. First, examine your results by looking at your monthly brokerage statements. Attempt to determine why you made the investments you did. This will let you know at once whether your investments were systematic or whether they were based on a whim, emotion, tips, rumors, fear, or greed. If you're like most investors, you'll find that a relatively small percentage of your investments were the result of a system, and that most of your investments were prompted by other factors, most of which were totally unrelated to any definitive system, method, or indicator.

This will alert you to a problem area in your investing. It will let you know, without a doubt, that you are not basing your decisions on a consistent approach. The second step, then, is to fix this problem by looking for a method that has simple, unambiguous rules of application.

MASTERING THE PSYCHOLOGICAL ASPECTS OF INVESTING

You can master the psychological end of investing by learning about yourself or by using simple, time-tested, mechanical techniques to overcome the problems. Purists would argue that the latter approach is shallow and not conducive to long-term change. I disagree.

Numerous mechanical techniques can be used to overcome problems of investor discipline. Whether the application of these mechanical methods results in permanent changes is irrelevant. If mechanical methods work, then I suggest you use them.

What do I mean by "mechanical methods"? Some of these are discussed in later chapters. Here are some examples:

- There are many investors who cannot follow their own rules. To overcome this limitation, simply turn your rules over to someone who will implement them for you.

- How about a method for helping investors who are too actively involved in (perhaps even addicted to) the markets? The answer is simple: Most overtrading comes from either too much contact with the market or attempting to follow too many markets or methods at the same time. A mechanical way of dealing with this problem is to eliminate the source or sources of information that stimulate you to make too many investments.

- Making a verbal contract with your broker can solve some of the problems.

Factors Underlying Successful Investing

Although there are many things an investor can do wrong in the markets, there are only a few things he or she can do right. We are all well aware of how important risk management, discipline, and a good investment method can be. Yet without a doubt, they are all useless in the hands of a trader who is psychologically inept or self-destructive. It is unfortunate that investors still believe in the myth that a better system will make them better investors.

The factors for achieving investment success are primarily psychological or behavioral. My experiences have taught me that three factors make up perhaps 90 percent of the formula for achieving and maintaining success:

1. *Detachment.* Many years ago, I learned that in order to invest successfully, I had to "not care," to be detached from my work as a trader. At times, being human gets in the way of success by throwing emotional roadblocks in your path. Emotional roadblocks cloud judgment and inhibit success. Just as a surgeon must not become emotionally involved with a patient, an investor must not become emotionally involved with his or her trades, or for that matter, with the idea of success. Keep yourself from caring too much, and you'll facilitate success.

2. *Persistence.* Clearly, the investor who is a quitter will never succeed, because he or she will not be in the markets when the big moves occur. A truly successful investor is willing to come back fighting after a loss or after a string of losses.

3. *Realistic attitude.* Investors must maintain a realistic attitude in order to succeed in the game of high expectations. All too often, investors have grossly unrealistic expectations about what they can achieve in the markets. Dreams of striking it rich or of being in on that one stock or property that makes you fabulously wealthy are self-destructive and divert your attention from the reality of your goal.

The fact of the matter is that you are far better off catching smaller profits that have a higher degree of accuracy than expecting large profits that are not likely to occur or will take so long to develop that you'll have at least 100 opportunities to make mistakes.

THE MAJORITY IS USUALLY WRONG— DON'T FORGET THAT!

There is a strong relationship between the level of market emotion and short-term market turns. When opinions are very optimistic, tops are likely; when opinions are very negative, bottoms are likely.

Remember these five general rules about investing and investor sentiment. They will serve you well!

1. Many investors lose money a majority of the time.

2. Most investors make incorrect decisions at major and minor market turning points.

3. When a majority of investors are in agreement that something will happen in the economy or in the market, they are usually incorrect.

4. The larger the degree of agreement, the more likely it is that a strongly held opinion will be incorrect.

5. It is more important to determine the opinions of average investors than those of professional traders.

If you want to learn more about trader psychology, I advise you to consult some of the resources listed at the end of this book. Above all, bear in mind that you, the investor, are the weakest link in the chain. No matter how potentially profitable your investment methods may be, they will be rendered totally useless or worse if you do not have the discipline to put them into action consistently according to the rules. *If there is only one thing you learn in this book, it is to have discipline.* You will *never succeed* without discipline.

I will give you more suggestions on how to improve your discipline and investor psychology. For now, the information I have given you should suffice. Now that you've survived the boring stuff, let's go on to Chapter 5, where the real fun begins.

CHAPTER FIVE

SETTING FINANCIAL GOALS

Larry works hard for his money. He can barely make ends meet in spite of the fact that he works a 50-hour week and another 10 hours on the weekend at a part-time job. He saves a few dollars each week, but the bulk of his money goes to pay bills and care for his family. By the time the bills are paid and the children are fed and clothed, the amount of money that remains is minimal. Larry believes that he will never have enough money to invest. The American dream is not his dream. After all, it takes money to make money, so if you don't have money you'll never strike it rich.

Larry has surveyed his choices. He can either continue to work to make ends meet or he can strike out on his own. But to start his own business, he has to have starting capital, unless he can find a business that requires hardly any start-up capital. Are there other alternatives? Yes, there are a few. Before you read about his choices, however, remember that there are many Larrys out there. To a certain extent, we are all Larry unless we have big money. Here are a few of Larry's choices:

- Given his limited finances and never-ending stream of expenses, Larry could get a third job. But what will happen to his quality of life? How will he continue to give his wife and children the time they need? How about his own enjoyment? Will he work three jobs for the rest of his life? When will the intensive effort end, giving Larry and his wife the time they want and need for a little enjoyment? Clearly, this is not a very appealing option.

- Larry's wife Ellen could get a full-time job in addition to her full-time job at home. What will that do to their relationship and their marriage? The stresses and strains are already substantial. And how will that affect the children? Will they have sufficient care and nurturing? Without a doubt this is not a positive alternative, although there are millions of married couples that find themselves in this situation given the cost of living in the United States.

- Perhaps Larry and Ellen could start their own business. This is indeed a very viable alternative and one that attracts many families. The good news is that Larry and his wife have their choice of quite a few home-based businesses. In fact, with the growth and development of Internet commerce, such ventures as selling merchandise via online auction sites can be a very good business. However, it is becoming a highly competitive area of commerce and takes skill and experience to make a profit. But this is true of all business ventures. Is there any bad news about starting your own business? It takes money, but the real issue is how much. More about this later.

- Larry could buy one of the many courses or seminars advertised on television, like zero-down real estate or some other business opportunity. Odds are that most of these will take more time, more money, and more effort than Larry wants to expend. Whether or not these business opportunities work will be discussed more fully in Chapter 8. Based on my understanding of these courses, it is unlikely they will work for you, or for Larry, in spite of what the promoters claim. The promoters of these courses make money on what is called the "up sell." Their initial offer is low priced and reasonable, and they often break even or lose money with the hope that they can sell you a higher-end product, course, or video seminar.

- Larry and his wife could take an entirely different direction and venture into the ultimate capitalist game: the stock market. They could become stock traders. To most people, this is the farthest thing from their minds. Yes, the proposition sounds scary, particularly if you have no idea what the stock market is or how you can make money in it. It can be intimidating. But then again, anything can be a challenge if you have no experience. There's no question you'll have to expend some effort if you're going to succeed. The good news and bad news of this alternative will be discussed more fully in Chapter 8.

- On a less aggressive level than being a stock trader, Larry and his wife could become investors. Investors are different from traders by a function of the time frame in which they conduct their business. The good news about this approach is that it proceeds slowly and steadily—and that's also the bad news. By this, I mean that it will take a long time before Larry and Ellen can build a reasonably large nest egg. And in the interim, their immediate financial crisis will not ease up at all. What they need is immediate relief—quick action and quicker results.

The situation I have just described is not unique. There are millions of individuals and families who struggle daily to make ends meet. The paradox of this situation is that there are more opportunities to acquire wealth today than ever before. Markets and business opportunities exist throughout the world and are often as close as your computer. The sad news is that the student who graduates college with a bachelor's degree will rarely make enough money to support an apartment, a car, car insurance, and a little money for entertainment and travel, let alone long-term investing or trading.

MANY INVESTORS HAVE BEEN LOSERS

If you're like most investors, you're either losing money or you're not making nearly as much as you should or could be making. Why? Because you're probably using the wrong methods, talking to the wrong people, listening to the wrong advice, or making the wrong decisions. The sad truth is that investors lose money not because they are ignorant but because they lack a plan and self-discipline. Here are some of their shortcomings. Do any of these sound familiar? Are they part of your behavior?

- *Too little capital and too big goals.* Most investors begin with too little capital and goals that are too ambitious. We have been told to aim high in order to achieve lofty goals, and this is indeed true. However, aiming high without the proper "ammunition" is an invitation for failure. Being realistic is a virtue when it comes to making your money grow. There is nothing wrong with a good sense of optimism, but it must be realistically tempered optimism. By the time you are done with this book, you will understand exactly what I mean by these comments.

■ *Failure to accept losses.* Ego is a powerful force that can work for or against individuals. Too many investors fail to take their losses when they have made a bad investment. They ride their losses for many months or even years. They often get out of their losing investments or trades when the market is bottoming, but only after sustaining losses for far too long.

■ *Buying stocks because they are "cheap."* This is yet another of the many blunders investors make. They incorrectly reason that buying a stock is not much different than buying real estate or a quality automobile. If a good home was selling for $300,000 last year and that same home is selling at $200,000 this year, and if there is nothing structurally or environmentally wrong with the home, odds are that it is indeed a good bargain. But there could be other problems that are not known to the buyer. There may be a new highway or airport construction project that will take over the area. Or there may be a street gang operating close by. In such cases, the investor might back away from what appears to be a bargain. The same holds true for stocks. If the stock of a major computer manufacturer had been trading at $65 per share and is now at $14 per share, there is a good reason for it. The mere fact that a stock was "worth" $100 a share three years ago does not mean that at $5 per share today it is worth anything. Remember that stocks are ultimately only worth the paper they are printed on. More about this in Chapters 8, 9, and 10.

- *Adding to a loss.* Many investors not only buy and hold stocks, even though they decline persistently, but they also compound the problem by adding to their losing investments. They reason that if the stock is a good buy at $40 per share, then it must be an even better bargain at $30 per share and a fantastic bargain at $10 per share. This approach is called *dollar cost averaging* (DCA). It will be discussed later. In and of itself, DCA is not a bad strategy, if you follow certain rules and if you have a large amount of money to invest. But for the new investor or trader, this is NOT a good strategy. One of the worst mistakes that investors make is to ride losses. Riding losses is a psychological problem that afflicts all investors and traders at one time or another. That's the bad news. The good news is that this, and other problems, can be overcome. My next point covers this problem in greater detail.

- *Emotional reactions are yet another problem.* The fact is that investors make decisions based on emotion and not on facts. Sadly, many investors want to sell when conditions appear to be the worst and buy when things appear to be the best. This happens because they are victims of their own insecurities. But what's worse is that they become victims of the news, the television business reports, brokerage house opinions, and world events. Joe Granville, the legendary stock market advisor, wisely stated that if something in the markets is obvious, then "it must obviously be wrong." Many times what may be apparent in the markets is not real. This problem alone is one of the most serious transgressions that the average investor commits. Yet, this difficulty is also surmountable.

- *Buying on tips and rumors.* Still another blunder that many investors make is to trade based on tips and rumors as opposed to solid strategies. They assume that if they got a great stock tip from their brother-in-law who has a client that knows someone who knows the president of a bio-technology firm that is going to come out with a new drug for treating cancer, that there must be money to be made in that stock. This is perhaps one of the most serious blunders that an investor can commit. And yet it happens every day to thousands if not millions of investors. No matter how disciplined you may be, there is always the temptation that a big winning investment will "fall in your laps." And though it may true that you are immune from such rash decisions most of the time, the one or two times that you fall victim to such panderings will cost you dearly. And this brings me to my next point: greed.

- *Greed.* Greed is another terrible emotion that causes investors to lose money. All too often, they believe that the stocks they own will become the biggest winners of the decade. When they are making money in a stock, they tend to believe that the gravy train will never end. They lose sight of reality, and then, when the stock begins to go down, they hold on in the belief that it will go back up again.

- *The need to hit home runs.* Many investors are in love with the fantasy that the stocks they buy will produce immense profits. The simple truth about investing and short-term trading is that you can achieve greater success hitting base hits and doubles than if you attempt to make a home run every time. Success is more a question of consistency than it is a question of infrequent, large moves. Some of the most successful investors have not made their big "killing" on one stock, but rather they have been consistent in their performance, making small but steady profits with a high level of accuracy. You will be far better off with small prof-

its and high accuracy than with large profits and low
accuracy.

- *Trying to do too much.* You are far better off being a special-
  ist in certain stocks or in certain types of investing than
  you are in attempting to be an expert at everything. Let's
  face it, there are hundreds of possibilities in the financial
  markets. You don't have the time or the expertise to do
  them all. Nor do you have the money to do it all! A simple, but highly recommended, rule of thumb is to find
  what works best for you and do it consistently. That's one
  of the keys to success! I advise you to focus on your investments rather than try to do too many things at one
  time. If you split your energies and your money into too
  many sectors, you will become a jack-of-all-trades but master of none.

- *Lack of organization.* Sadly, too many investors are disorganized. They fail to keep their market homework up-to-
  date, forget about or avoid tracking their investments,
  forget to put orders in when required to do so, and keep
  terrible records. Although none of these may seem especially important in and of themselves, when several such
  blunders are combined, the net result can be costly. Disorganization can cause investors to miss opportunities and
  turn winning trades into losers. Clearly, this does not contribute to the goal of making money. Many tools are available to avoid the problems that disorganization can create,
  but be sure to use them to your advantage. There are few
  things that will cause you as much distress as losing money
  due to disorganization or errors of oversight.

These are some of the reasons that investors tend to lose
money in the stock market. Can losing behavior be reversed?

Can the average person learn how to invest and make money in the stock market? The answer is an emphatic "YES"! This book will teach you some of the strategies you'll need to know, but more than that, it will acquaint you with other strategies and profit-making opportunities to help you no matter what your age or how much money you have to invest.

VICTIMS OF THE SYSTEM

Let's face it, we're all victims of the financial monopoly. The big-shot money managers, real estate moguls, franchise marketers, bankers, and brokerage firms have been shaping and molding our minds for years. They've filled our heads with the information they want us to believe. They groom us and fatten us up for the kill, like cattle in a feedlot. There's no conspiracy here, just the old boys' network in the world of investing. Never has this been as evident as it is today in the early 2000s. Brokerage houses, financial analysts, and investment advisors have been implicated in all sorts of tricks and schemes designed to separate the trading public from its money. A number of brokerage houses and some of their top analysts have knowingly touted worthless stocks, given certain clients favorable treatment, maintained high ratings on stocks that they knew were essentially worthless, and generally misled the public. It's no wonder that investors have lost confidence in the system.

Rest assured that such tricks are not unique to the stock and futures markets. No matter what the area of financial focus may be, there is an insiders' network that benefits from the best deals. In order for you, the average individual, to make money in the stock market, real estate market, franchise market, futures market, or any other area, you need to learn how to think for yourself, act on your own, and avoid depending on anyone else.

If you have the patience and the time, this book will show you how to work outside the old boys' club to make good profits without becoming a victim of their schemes and games. The rules you will learn beginning in this chapter will be highly valuable to you no matter which areas you decide to focus on.

A FEW GENERAL RULES TO GET YOU STARTED

Clearly, you have many choices at your disposal. As I noted in the preceding pages, you can spend your time and money on many different schemes. In the long run, you will likely find that most of these will be either out-and-out scams, difficult if not impossible to apply, or just plain useless. You will have wasted time, effort, and money. And to make things worse, you'll probably feel like you've been taken advantage of—and you very likely have been. Adding insult to injury, you may be contacted again by these marketing firms and may fall victim to yet another scheme designed to separate you from your money. Finally, you'll be added to the sucker list, and before you know it, you'll be getting all types of solicitations in the mail, e-mail, and telephone.

If you are truly interested in learning a skill that will serve you well, not only in your financial life and future but also in your personal life, then pay attention to what I have to say. In the final analysis, even after having learned the tools in this book, your success will depend on three skills you will need to possess if you truly want to make big bucks. These skills are:

1. *Persistence.* Although I will expound on this at length later, suffice it to say that you will need to come back and try again after every failure. The methods I will teach you are not perfect; they do not work 100 percent of the time. But after a few successive failures, the next attempt will

likely work. If you give up after a few defeats, you won't be around for the sweet victory and the money that comes with it. Computer testing and experience with investment results clearly indicate that even the most effective investment approaches lose money at least 30 percent of the time. In fact, some methods that are highly successful in the long run frequently have even lower levels of accuracy. Finally, some of the most effective investment strategies are incorrect as many as seven times in a row. What does that tell us? Simply, we need to be patient, persistent, and willing to accept a series of losses if we are going to be successful in the long run.

2. *Self-discipline.* The ability to persist is a variation on the theme of self-discipline. I have stated, perhaps even overstated, the importance of discipline on many occasions throughout this book. Even if you only have one hour a week to spend on your financial future (because you're working so hard at other jobs to pay the bills), you'll have to spend that one hour religiously, with self-discipline, in order to get the results you want. In addition, you'll need courage, strength, and guts to take the necessary actions at the required times. The best-planned strategy is totally useless unless you have the courage and self-discipline to put it into action and follow it through to its conclusion.

3. *Self-control.* Self-control is, in actuality, a form of self-discipline. Self-control will be your greatest ally on the road to profitable investing. Without the ability to control your emotions and avoid being a victim of the media, the news, your friends' opinions, or your own insecurity, you will need to develop and put into action your self-control. At times, you will have to ignore what may appear to be

obvious and take affirmative action in a financially risky plan. Some of your best money will likely be made when you feel the most fear and pessimism. Some of your worst losses will occur when you are confident, self-assured, and convinced that your strategy cannot fail.

Armed with these three skills (which you will need to develop as fully as possible), you will be more certain of success in your ventures and adventures. In addition to the above, here is a pre-liminary list of things to do in order to facilitate your journey on the road to success. Although it is certainly possible to make big money without following these rules, the odds will be greatly in your favor if you take the actions I have listed below. You might find it helpful to make a copy of this list and check off those that you already do and those that you need to put into action.

One last thing before I give you the list: Some of what I sug-gest will not be palatable to you, your family, or your friends. You may find that people are not pleased with your new attitude and your new way of doing things. If that's the case, be polite and tell them you've turned over a new leaf. There is no need to flaunt your new wisdom and methods; that will only alienate them and make them insecure. Remember above all that they aren't the one who will pay your bills, put your children through college, or buy you that big house, fast car, or fancy boat you've been craving. The game of making money is often a solitary adven-ture. You will also find that when success comes to you, it will be much easier to discern friend and foe. Don't be too surprised if people that you thought were your friends turn on you because of their jealousies. And don't be too surprised if people who ap-peared to be either casual acquaintances or seemingly disinter-ested suddenly take an interest in you. When you develop the skills I am about to teach you, your personal life and many of your attitudes may change.

Here is my list of suggestions. Take your time, study them, and then put them into action. You may not agree with all of my suggestions but, at the very minimum, give them the attention and consideration they deserve. They are based on my more than 30 years of experience, during which I have had my successes *and* my failures. I've learned more from my failures than I have from my successes. If you pay attention to me, you will decrease your learning time significantly. Finally, remember that if you don't "get" all of this the first time, I'll be expanding on these ideas throughout the course of this book.

Throw out those worthless stock reports. When it comes to quality investment advice, you often get what you pay for. Some of the best advice from top-notch analysts with superb performance records is either unavailable to the average investor of limited funds or too expensive to justify a small investment portfolio. On the other hand, literally hundreds of investment newsletters offer free advice with the promise (and at times what appears to be a guarantee) that you will make money following their advice.

In addition, if you have managed to get your name on Internet mailing lists or fax lists (which includes most of us these days), you will likely be bombarded daily with e-mail. Many tout stock services and even individual stocks. If you fall victim to these promotions, you will likely lose money in the long run. The simple fact is that most of this advice is totally worthless.

If you're already a stock market investor, then do yourself a big favor and trash those worthless stock reports. If you're a new investor, don't even open those seductive e-mails. Generally, they will be wrong as often as they are right. The ultimate goal of such reports is to generate a commission, support a stock in which the writer or writers have a vested interest, or promote a stock as part of a paid public relations campaign. Typically, such reports will not tell you when to buy or sell; they merely tell you to buy. They also don't assist you with timing. *Timing is a key element in the equation for success.* Once you have decided what to buy or sell, you will need to know when to buy or sell. This book will teach you how to time your investments. So, do yourself a big favor and don't even look at those reports or you may get tempted into what will more often than not turn out to be a costly blunder.

If you are not already an investor, don't make the mistake of reading these reports. The reports I'm referring to, of course, are any of the free opinions and recommendations offered by brokerage houses, Web sites, or e-mail that flows endlessly into your mailbox.

Ignore analyst opinions. Analysts are employed by brokerage houses. Their job is to analyze stocks and advise brokerage house clients and/or the public whether given stocks are worth buying, selling, or holding. Although many analysts are competent, honest, and care about investors, the sad truth is that a handful of dishonest analysts have placed the entire profession and procedure of analyst recommendations in a bad light. The continued buy recommendations in worthless stocks by analysts from the late 1990s until early 2002, as these stocks literally crashed, is a glaring example of what can happen if investors allow themselves to be manipulated by those who purport to be professionals in their areas of expertise. Although most brokerage houses have taken steps to separate their research departments from brokerage commission and sales departments, the truth is that any analyst on the payroll of a brokerage firm has a vested interest and can therefore be influenced by the desires and directions of the firm. I do not believe that any measures short of complete independence of market analysts will serve the purpose of creating the needed credibility.

I suggest that unless an analyst is totally independent and has a lengthy track record of successful stock picks and honesty, you ignore his or her opinions. Be especially suspicious of guest experts who give their opinions on business television. Most of these individuals are employees of, directors of, shareholders in, or otherwise associated with firms that stand to benefit in one way or another from their recommendations and/or television appearances. The popular CNBC cable television business station and many others have instituted a policy of asking guests whether they own any of the stocks they are recommending or discussing and whether their firm owns any of the stocks. Such questions may give a false sense of security to the public, because they do not sufficiently address the basic issues:

- Are they being paid to tout the stocks?

- Does anyone in their families stand to benefit from their recommendations?

- Do they intend to buy or sell the stocks they have discussed?

- Do they have a reciprocal arrangement with other firms or individuals to recommend stocks in which they have a vested interest?

These are more specific and useful questions, ones that you will not see asked or answered on any of the business television shows. Regardless of disclosures, it is unlikely you will be able to fully trust most of the opinions you get on television from either analysts or advisors. The sad fact is that the vast majority of them have poor track records. Their opinions are usually worthless.

Recently, commentators on many business television programs have become market experts. Several have written investment books and regularly tout them on the air to a ready-made audience. Sadly, at least one of these books has been roundly critiqued as generally worthless and even inaccurate. The investing public seems to believe that just because someone on television is giving advice it is worthwhile. Don't get me wrong. Some of the guests and even some of the commentators on CNBC, Bloomberg, and CNN are quite accomplished and competent. However, as a new investor, you will not know this and may take seriously investment advice from those who are not skilled or sufficiently experienced.

Don't bother with the ultimate franchise opportunity. I indicated earlier that although you *can* make money in ventures other than the stock market, odds are you'll need considerable working capital to take advantage of the good ones, and you'll need to put a great deal of effort into the program. *Unless you already have a good nest egg to begin with, you won't be able to get into the good franchise opportunities.* If you're looking for a franchise opportunity, it would be best to take your time, accumulate money from your other investments, and then diversify into a potentially profitable franchise.

Forget about making a killing in special-events T-shirts. This warning is just another way of saying what I've said before: Any of the "get rich quick on a shoestring budget" schemes has a low probability of success. I am not saying that you won't do well with a novel business idea, but the problem with such ideas is that they take time and money to develop and many more fail than succeed. Furthermore, if you've developed a clever idea, the odds are high that the idea will be copied or stolen from you unless it is capable of being fully protected by copyright or patent.

Stop listening to Uncle Joe. Uncle Joe is my symbol for the well-intentioned tipster who thinks he or she is doing you a favor by telling you what stocks to buy. My advice is to tune out all the tips, no matter who has given them to you. In all probability, the tips you get will come from people who know less about stocks than you do. They are laboring under the misconception that making money in the stock market is the result of tips and inside information. If they indeed knew anything about the markets, they wouldn't be passing on tips or rumors, and they certainly wouldn't be telling other people their supposedly valuable information. Be especially suspicious of family members who tell you that they "know someone who knows someone else who is the cousin of a friend's wife who is closely connected to the president of a company that has a new product that is top secret." Those kinds of tips are invitations to losing money and rarely work out. Yet, it is human nature to give and take stock tips. You may need to learn a few costly lessons before you believe me.

Rely only on yourself and the resources you have identified as credible. Best of all, these fantastic resources won't cost you a penny! The best way for you to make money in the stock market is to rely on your own good efforts and the application of the tools you will learn in this book. The concept is a simple one indeed: If you depend on yourself, then you will have no one to thank for your successes and no one to blame for your failure(s) other than yourself. The whole idea behind this book is to teach you a skill that will work for you, independent of what anyone else can sell you, tell you, or give you.

Set aside a certain amount of time to this project. Unless you are willing to set aside a certain amount of time to learning what is in this book, you might as well not begin. You will be wasting your time if you go into this venture without a commitment, a lack of time, or a lack of motivation. You can change your financial future for the better, but only with effort and persistence. Even if you can only give your plan 15 minutes a week, do it consistently, without distractions and without interruptions. I suggest that you schedule the time and stick to your schedule diligently. Give the concepts in this book a fighting chance. It will only cost you a little time and a little money to see if this is the right approach for you.

Once you have learned the basics, go on to the more advanced applications. You will see as you progress through this book that I have provided a number of ways and numerous suggestions that can help you make money. Some of the more advanced methods require more starting capital and cannot be applied until you have achieved some degree of success with the preliminary approaches. Therefore, it is not really necessary for you to learn them immediately. However, as soon as you realize that success is on its way, read the chapters that pertain to longer-term financial growth, stability, and retirement planning. If you are a young person, you have a distinct advantage over those who are considerably older than you but who are only now beginning to make their fortunes. The younger you are when you begin, the more money you can make and the better your odds of success.

Try not to read the business newspapers or business magazines. Clearly this information is contrary to what you will read or may have read elsewhere. I am certain that my suggestion will arouse the ire of many who do not feel as I do about investing. Consider that we have been brainwashed to believe that the more information we have about stocks, the more likely will be our chances of success. Unfortunately, recent history has proven that even the most credible and thorough information can be incorrect or tainted. Companies have been practicing tricky or outright misleading reporting practices with their earnings reports for years. Recently, the use of pro forma earnings projections and reports has fooled many an investor, because these reports ignore or fail to contain vital information about the debts of a company.

We have all been told time and again that in order to make money we need information. We have been led to believe that if we have more information, then we will do well. I respectfully submit that this is not the case. Too much information can be confusing and can lead you astray.

THE "BORING" PART OF SETTING FINANCIAL GOALS

Setting goals can often be boring and tedious. Few of us want to think 30 years into the future. In fact, many of us can't visualize what we'll be doing 30 years from now or where we'll be doing it. One thing is for certain—no matter where we'll be, what we'll be doing, or how we'll be doing it, we'll need money to do it. And the more of it we have, the better off we'll be.

Don't get me wrong. It isn't entirely about money! It's also about enjoying the limited amount of time we have been given on earth. But what about the next life? What about reincarnation? What about the spiritual you? Seeking financial freedom has nothing to do with these! There's nothing mutually exclusive here. You can choose to be a Buddhist like Richard Gere and still have big bucks. You can become a scientologist like John Travolta and still have a ton of money.

Remember that our goal is to lay the groundwork for financial success. As such, we will deal with finances, perhaps at times in mercenary ways. But don't let my approach lead you to believe that I am an unfeeling person who is interested in money alone. Nor should you assume that being entirely focused on money and success to the exclusion of feelings are prerequisites to profit. They are not. You need to develop your spiritual and feeling sides as well. Money in the absence of friends, family, and effective relationships is totally useless. Please remember that!

Be your own financial planner. Do you really need an expert? What does a financial planner do? Simply stated, a financial planner examines your assets, liabilities, needs, skills, earning power, and goals, within the framework of available investment tools. The planner then develops a program or method for you that is supposed to help you achieve your goals within the time frame you have set for yourself. In short, a financial planner gives you direction within the limits of what you can do currently. Certainly, as you grow older and develop new skills, it will be necessary for you to update your financial plan. Yet, if you are just beginning your venture into the world of profits and investing, then it is unlikely that a financial planner can help you at all. You'll probably be told to come back when you have some money. So what can you do? Here are a few ideas for you:

- If you're just getting started, don't even bother with a financial planner. Make your own plans by following my suggestions in this chapter.

- If you've already made some money from your investments and you're saving money, you will want to make a plan on your own, again, following the guidelines provided in this chapter.

- Take advantage of the Internet. There are many Web sites that offer quality advice and recommendations on financial planning. In fact, several—such as <http://financialplan.about.com/>—offer financial planning courses so you can be your own financial planner.

- Remember that you won't have to be too concerned about financial planning until you have made some money from your investments.

- Finally, bear in mind that a solid financial plan must also include tax planning, so that you can keep more for yourself and pay less in taxes (as long as the strategies you use are legal).

In addition to the Web site listed above, note the following Internet locations where you can find considerable information and assistance on financial planning—in most cases, free of charge:

- http://financialplan.about.com/

- www.kiplinger.com/

- www.ihatefinancialplanning.com/homepage.jsp

- http://learningforlife.fsu.edu/course/fp101/index.html

- www.efmoody.com/planning/planningoverview.html

- www.e-analytics.com/fpdir1.htm

- http://moneycentral.msn.com/planning/home.asp

- http://directory.google.com/Top/Home/Personal_Finance/

Determine your goals in 15 minutes or less. You can easily determine your financial goals quickly and without too much deliberation. In order to make your efforts worthwhile, you should attempt to make at least 25 percent profit on your money per year. If you can safely do so year after year, then you will be way ahead of the game after ten years. More realistically, however, there will be years in which you will make less and, in fact, years in which you will actually lose money. Here is a realistic road map for you to follow if you're just getting started:

1. *First year—expect to break even.* This will be your year to learn, to make mistakes, and to break old losing habits. While it may take you a year to achieve this goal, it could take less or more time depending on your discipline and commitment to the program.

2. *Second year—you should have learned enough the first year to make at least 15 percent on your money.* As a rule of thumb, you should be able to generate at least twice as much as you can earn in the bank. When the economy is in an inflationary trend, you should do especially well, beating the rate of inflation handily.

3. *Third year—your investment program should be returning good profits to you, provided you have been able to maintain your discipline and investment approach.* If you are not successful after the third year, odds are you have done something dreadfully wrong or do not understand the principles in this book.

4. *Fourth year—once you have spent three years learning the methods suggested in this book, you will be able to go off on your own.* In other words, you may have gotten enough experience by now to have developed and tested your own ideas.

When you make your financial plan, you must consider whether you plan to have (or already have) children and estimate the cost of raising them through graduate school. While you may think it is unreasonable to see your children through graduate school, this is a worst-case scenario. In other words, assume that your children will not be able to contribute anything to their education and that they will receive no scholarships or other assistance. The worst-case scenario is often the right thing for you to assume, because doing so will help you know what you're up against.

Five simple steps to help you set realistic and attainable financial goals. Here are five specific tips to help you set realistic financial goals:

1. *Make a true and honest assessment of your assets and liabilities.* Take a look at how much money you have in the bank, how much you're worth in earning power, and how much you pay out monthly in living expenses. The bottom line figure is what is called your disposable income (DI). As an example, consider the following:

   Annual income after taxes: $37,500
   Monthly rent, utilities: $785 × 12 months = $9,420
   Monthly food, gas, travel: $375 × 12 months = $4,500
   Monthly car and insurance: $385 × 12 months = $4,620
   Monthly miscellaneous expenses: $250 × 12 months = $3,000
   Total expenses: $21,540
   Disposable income: $15,960

2. *Take 15 percent of your bottom line disposable income as the amount that you can afford to invest.* In the example above, you would have roughly $2,300 to invest, barring any unforeseen expenses. To be conservative, you would take even less, perhaps 10 percent or in this case about $1,500 as the amount you would initially invest.

3. *Depending on the method you decide to use as your investment approach, you will commit about one-tenth the amount monthly or the entire amount at once.*

4. *Do not spend any of the profits you make.* Put your profits back into your investment program.

5. *As the income from your job increases, you will have more money to put into your investments.* Make certain you monitor your DI yearly, if not more often—every three months, for instance.

The dangers of setting unrealistic goals. Much has been said about the virtues of having lofty goals. Although it's a good idea to have high expectations, the truth is that you can only attain goals that are realistic. There's a big difference between having an optimistic objective and frustrating yourself with a goal that you can't possibly attain. Success at small goals is better than failure at large goals, and these will bolster your positive attitude. As you gain experience and confidence, you can set higher goals, but at first, your goal should be to make a profit. Be happy with a profit, even if that profit is small.

The dangers of setting goals that are too easily achieved. On the other hand, once you have gained some experience, you will want to set your goals a little higher. As an example, it is fairly easy to make a few dollars a day as a day trader in stocks, but the bottom line is that a few dollars a day is not worth your time and trouble. You can probably do better working for $6 an hour at the local hamburger stand. While setting small goals is good at first, it will not serve you well once you have learned how to make money. Raise your goals considerably after you feel confident with the methods you have learned.

What to do when you have reached your initial goals. Once you have reached your initial goals, you can think about diversification. If you have been successful in mutual funds, then consider trading individual stocks. If you have had success in individual stocks, then consider trading stock options, single stock futures, or futures. And, if you have done well with any or all of these vehicles, you can consider options strategies.

Take baby steps at first. Obviously, taking small steps when you get started is better. I will provide you with specific instructions on how to do this when I introduce each of the investment methods to you in subsequent chapters. Following are some questions to ponder:

- Being a consistent base hitter is preferable to being an inconsistent home run hitter—what's wrong with a .350 batting average?

- Being highly accurate or being highly profitable—which is best for you?

- Would you rather reach your goals with high odds of success or with erratic strokes of luck?

- Investing versus gambling—where do you stand?

- How do your attitudes affect your goals?

- How do you shut out the brainwashing and lock in the solid strategies that will take you to your goals?

- What is your unconventional checklist for goal setting?

The next chapter will tear down many of the misconceptions you may have about investing, replacing them with ideas that have not been polluted by the investment establishment and the society in which we live. Get ready for an exciting and profitable ride!

CHAPTER SIX

THE GENERAL INVESTMENT MODEL

AN OVERVIEW OF THE GENERAL INVESTMENT MODEL (GIM)

This chapter will serve as your introduction to an investment approach that has the potential to help you realize your goal of financial independence. As you know from having read the preceding five chapters, I am a firm believer in the importance of organization, discipline, effective investor psychology, and thorough planning. If you want to achieve success, you will follow my rules; however, if you want to gamble or "take a shot," you don't need this book. If I have laid the groundwork correctly, this chapter will help bring things together for you. But don't stop here!

The investment model I will teach you in this chapter is one of two important steps. Learning and internalizing this model will *not* guarantee success, however. The model can help you understand investing in general, but as you know, understanding and knowing *how* to do something are two entirely different things. A good teacher is not necessarily a good practitioner, and conversely, a good practitioner may not necessarily be a good teacher. Regardless, make a commitment to learn and put into practice the general investment approach discussed in this chapter.

The General Investment Model (GIM) is an approach I have developed based on my many years of experience. Don't let the title of this model scare you; it's a very easy model to follow. In fact, you may like it so much that you'll want to follow it in other areas of your life, because it's very sensible and cuts through much of the nonsense that hinders making decisions about investments. If you consider relationships to be investments, which I believe they are, then you may find this model useful here, too.

The GIM provides you with a framework or structure within which to base your decisions. Without such a framework, you will surely be lost and may make bad decisions. Consider the GIM your first step in the investing process. Unless you are very lucky, you will not be able to make money or have a successful relationship with your investments without such a model. The GIM is only one of several investment approaches that can help you achieve success. I favor this method above all others, because it is simple to understand, easily applicable to all types of investments, simple to teach, and very logical.

Although some people will disagree with my view, I can assure you that I have found it very helpful; it has opened the eyes of many thousands of people I have taught over the past 25 years. In view of its major importance, I suggest that you study it carefully and that you apply it as often as you can. In so doing, you will see that it is not only sensible but effective. As a matter of fact, you may want to view some of your previous investment decisions within the context of this approach. When you do, you will be able to see where you went wrong and what you did that was right. The GIM will help you avoid errors, while at the same time maximizing your profits. Perhaps I am overstating my case, but I will remind you that unless you learn the GIM and the timing method presented in Chapter 7, you will likely fail in your efforts to become financially independent.

The GIM is divided into five parts:

1. Historical pattern

2. Expectation

3. Confirmation

4. Action

5. Management

While this model may not sound exciting to you at first, I think you'll change your mind when you see the flowchart of the GIM in Figure 6.1 and a few examples.

Each step in the GIM is dependent on the successful completion of the previous step. If any step in the model is skipped or incorrect, the entire model will fail and you will lose money. If you correctly follow each step, you may still lose money, but your odds of making money are considerably higher than if you

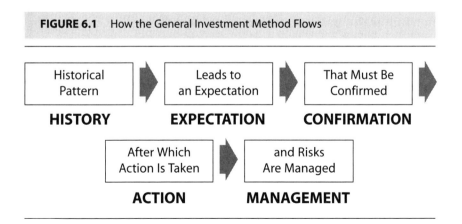

FIGURE 6.1   How the General Investment Method Flows

do not follow the model at all. Each step in the model is fully explained below.

Now let's take a look at the aspects of the GIM. Remember to keep an open mind and focus on the logic of what I'm saying—*not* on the ultimate application. And while you are doing this, I suggest that you clear your mind of what you may have learned elsewhere, because it will only confuse you.

Historical Pattern

What do I mean when I talk about a historical pattern? The simple answer is that every investment, every stock, every market, real estate, and relationships all have patterns. What is a pattern? There are literally hundreds of patterns in our daily lives and in the financial markets. Such patterns consist of repetitive price cycles, seasonality, day-of-week relationships, and market indicators. As an investor, you will want to follow the most basic patterns; however, as a preliminary example, consider the cyclical pattern in the stock market as shown in Figure 6.2.

The chart shows the four-year cycle pattern in the U.S. stock market. As you can see, this pattern has run about four years in length from one price low to another. While the stock market does not follow the pattern perfectly, it does track quite closely. The idea of using a pattern is to help you get close to a turning point in the market. Patterns help you develop an expectation. It is entirely possible that your expectation will change as time passes. Remember that expectations are not realities and need to be confirmed. Don't take any action until an expectation is confirmed.

As long as you know what to do with the expectation, you will fare well; however, if you allow the expectation to overcome your good judgment, then you will lose money in your investments. This is a very important point! Please remember it in all you do.

FIGURE 6.2   The Four-Year Cycle in S&P Futures. This cycle chart shows my evaluation of the ideal approximate lows and highs of this pattern. As you can see, a cycle low was projected for late 2002 if the pattern is on time.

Created with TradeStation by Omega Research ® 1997

An expectation is NOT a reality. It merely points you in a direction, telling you what MIGHT happen. Never let your expectation of what MIGHT happen become transformed into the belief that it WILL happen. The outcome of an investment is never a certainty, and as long as you remember this, you will do well. This brings me to the next major topic—expectation.

Expectation

As I told you earlier, if you allow your expectation to influence you to the point of believing that it MUST become a reality, then you are surely headed for trouble. Here is an example of what I mean. Many investors believe that gold is a good thing to own in the event that there is political or economic instability, either at home or anywhere in the world. The idea that gold might be a good protective investment in such cases is a good one. Yet, the facts indicate that for many years gold has not been a good investment. Some people believe that whenever an international situation threatens to escalate or encourage instability, their best defense is to buy gold mining stocks or gold in the form of coins. Their expectation, based on history, may be a good one. Their reasoning is sound, but it is based on the belief that international conflict or domestic problems always (or most often) cause the price of gold to go up. In actuality, this is *not* the case, because the situation is not that simple. The relationship between conflict, economic instability, inflation, or deflation and the price of gold is not 100 percent predictable.

When investors buy gold in anticipation of a crisis escalating, and the price of gold fails to go up when the crisis actually develops, then the only reasonable action is to get out of gold because the expectation, based on a historical belief, failed to materialize. Yet, investors—especially in gold—often refuse to get out when their expectation fails to develop into a reality. They keep their gold as it declines for many days, months, and even years. They tie up their capital in a nonproductive investment, because they are convinced that their expectations will become a reality. And when the expectation fails to materialize, they refuse to abandon their ideas, failing to take their loss or break even.

This is only one very small example of what happens when you allow an expectation to negatively affect your thinking and your actions. Perhaps the most glaring example of such a situation was the recent Y2K bug and the "end of the world" hysteria that surrounded the coming of the 21st century. If you think back to that situation, you will recall that supposedly knowledgeable individuals in the government, scientists, economists, financial advisors, and the clergy all warned us of what might happen. While many individuals in positions of authority were moderate and acted sensibly so as not to alarm the public, others went on highly visible campaigns that literally scared the stuffing out of investors. These individuals advocated selling all stocks and the stockpiling of food, medical supplies, energy sources, and weapons. The predictions seem laughable, now that we look back on them. Still, there are those who made major preparations, who sold their homes, stocked up on supplies, changed their investments, and closed their bank accounts. And when 2000 came and went with virtually no problems at all, they stubbornly remained with their losing positions, because they allowed their expectations to rule their sensibilities and failed to admit to their folly.

Confirmation

This brings us to the cure for expectation—confirmation. Yes, once we have developed an expectation based on historically valid patterns, we must have a method by which we confirm that the given expectations will become a reality. We need a method by which to improve the odds of our expectation actually developing into the situation we had anticipated. There are a number of ways in which this can be achieved, ranging from the very simple to the highly technical. I will discuss confirmation methods in detail in Chapter 7.

Action

Taking action is the next step in the sequence. Without action, nothing will happen. Yes, it's true that you can't lose money if you don't take action, but it's also true that you won't make money. This step in the sequence of the GIM is one of the most critically important, because it is in taking action or failing to do so that many investors blunder. Taking action sounds like a simple thing to do, but in reality it is very complex and calls into play a host of psychological factors. We know from our previous readings here that investor psychology is a fragile thing. We know that, in fact, psychology is the weakest link in the chain. This is why I have devoted considerable space throughout this book to help you overcome the limitations of your own psychology.

The process of taking action is, in fact, so intricate and subject to errors at every turn that an entire book could be written on the topic. Consider the following issues:

- Why do we fail to take action when we have a very good sense of what is likely to happen?

- Why do we take action too soon or too late?

- Why do we allow others to sway our decisions to take action?

- Do we have trouble getting out of an investment after we have followed through perfectly?

- What causes the fear that prevents action?

- What causes the greed that causes us to act too soon?

- Why do we take actions that are too aggressive or too meek?

- Why are we nervous when we take action?

- Why are we overly confident when we take action?

As you can see, taking action is a very important part of the General Investment Model, one that is rarely given attention in other books on investing. Far too many writers in this field believe that people will follow through as they should. Reality teaches us that this is not the case, that people don't follow through. *Reality tells us that the best methods of investing will be rendered useless by investors who fail to take action, take incorrect actions in spite of the information they have at hand, or somehow alter the course of action, causing it to fail.* Unless an investment book or course addresses this vital topic, I believe the teaching is glaringly incomplete, perhaps even counterproductive.

Management

I assume you have understood and effectively followed the first four parts of the GIM and that you have made a profit on your investment. What do you do now? The answer is simple but specific: You must manage the profit effectively—either by taking the money and turning the paper profit into an actual profit or by holding on to the investment and setting up new possibilities or alternatives based on how the investment continues to perform. If your investment now shows a loss, you need to manage the loss by not allowing it to become so large as to deplete all of your available capital or tie up your money indefinitely while you wait for the loss to become smaller or even turn into a profit. Here are some of the issues we will address in this area of the GIM:

- When should you take your profit?

- When should you take your loss and call it quits?

- How much of a loss is acceptable?

- How much profit should you anticipate?

- When should you add to your investment positions?

■ How can you prevent a profit from turning into a loss?

■ How long should you wait for a loss to turn into a profit?

■ When and how do you know when you made a wrong decision?

These are all important issues that are rarely addressed in most books on investing. I will attempt to give you specific answers to these questions in Chapters 7 through 10, so you can increase the chances of your success and lessen your failures.

Next, let's see how the General Investment Model applies to the major issues that this book addresses.

How to Plan for Your Future Using the GIM

In order to plan effectively for your future NOW, learn the details of my General Investment Model until you know them backwards and forwards. Become totally familiar with the limitations of each step as well as the issues you will encounter in implementing each step. Don't allow yourself to be dissuaded by the fact that you don't have enough money. To have more later, you have to begin with something *now*. I have outlined the four steps you need to take, in order to get started on the road to financial independence:

1. *Get a firm grip on how much money you have to invest.* Some of the things you will need to do in order to complete this step have already been discussed in Chapters 3, 4, and 5. If you don't have the patience to follow through in detail with my suggestions, then at the very least develop a general idea of how much money you plan to start with. I don't care if it's $50 or $50,000, as long as you make a commit-

ment. *Learn the General Investment Model and examine a few hypothetical investments within the context of the GIM.*

2. *Decide on which area or areas of investment make the most sense to you within your budget.* Clearly, someone who has $500 cannot realistically make a commitment in the real estate market, regardless of the claims made by the "zero money down" people. Yes, you can become creative and make deals, but this approach is beyond the scope of this book. If you want to become a wheeler-dealer, then I refer you to the excellent example of Donald Trump and his book, *The Art of the Deal.*

3. *Take the first step and make an investment.* Although I advocate action, I do not mean that any action will be better than no action. The major portion of this book is devoted to taking action, but remember that you do not need to become obsessive in making a decision. Frequently, you will have a number of choices, any of which will be good as a starting point. Again, I want to emphasize that *action* is one of the keys to success. While there are many things you can do that are wrong and that will surely lead to losses, the good news is that there are also many things you can do that will be correct. Some may be more profitable than others, but you need to jump into the water and begin swimming.

4. *And finally, you must change your perceptions.* Now that sounds like a tall order. How can you possibly do this? It's easy, and it's difficult. If you have allowed yourself to slip into the perception of poverty, then you will continue to think like a poor person. You will lack self-confidence and motivation, and you will fail to see opportunities when they present themselves. You will see yourself in a nega-

tive light, and this will clearly affect your motivation. There are many things you can do to overcome negative perception. I could easily recommend a dozen books that will help you, but the best way to change your perception is to take a chance and to succeed. Nothing changes attitudes and perceptions like good old profits!

THE SETUP, TRIGGER, AND FOLLOW-THROUGH METHOD (STF)

I have already discussed the importance of following a definitive investment model such as the GIM, which is an important tool because it provides a structure for making decisions and evaluating potential investments. The GIM applies to all investments, whether stocks, mutual funds, options, or real estate. The concept is simple but powerful. Learn it, and it will serve you well. Ignore it, and eventually you will come back to it when you realize that it would not only have saved you money but would have made you money as well!

While all aspects and phases of the GIM are important, the actual process of making an investment decision is the most important, because it is the *action* portion of the formula. Taking action is vital to success, but taking action prematurely or too late can spell disaster. Unfortunately, too many investors fail to take action when the time is right; this holds true for experienced investors as well as newcomers. In order to assist you with the decision-making process that leads to action, I have developed another model that operates within the GIM. This submodel or set of rules will help you know when to "pull the trigger." In other words, it will help you know when the time is right to actually take action or when you must wait.

You may recall that I emphasized the importance of avoiding the pitfall of equating expectations with realities, that just because you expect something to happen does not mean it will. *This is a significant distinction to be given serious consideration at all times.* Do not make the mistake that so many investors make. Do not allow an expectation to take on the role of a reality, unless the expectation is confirmed or validated by actual events or other methods, which you will learn as you continue reading.

At this time, I would like to show you a three-step process that leads to action. Note that this approach is applicable to any form of investment. I call it the "setup, trigger, and follow-through" approach, or the STF method. Here are several examples of the STF approach, which I believe will drive my point home fully. If you don't follow my logic at first, please go back and read these examples again. Once you understand the STF method, you will see investing in a whole new light. I believe this new view promises to open doors in virtually all areas of your life, investment and otherwise.

Example 1: Premature Action Based on Faulty Evaluation of Reality

Your boss sends you an e-mail requesting to meet with you as soon as possible. You don't like the tone of the message. Previous similar communications from your boss have all been indicative of problems for which you were reprimanded. You conclude from the tone of the e-mail and the terseness of the message, that you are headed for trouble. You feel justified in being concerned, because the history of such communications has always meant trouble for you.

I call this portion of the experience the *setup*. Based on your experience, you believe you are being set up or prepared for a bad experience. You believe that this is the first step to a bad outcome for you. And your conclusion is reasonable; however, you need more proof. What if this isn't the setup you expected? What if this time the outcome is a positive one? What if your boss normally has a negative attitude or tone, whether he or she is angry or not? How would you know when your boss is pleased with your work if you have not yet experienced that behavior under such conditions? What if the boss used a form letter? What if he or she has an intimidating style simply to assert his or her position of power? There are many other possibilities, but you won't even consider them because you have already gone beyond the *reality* of the e-mail. And the conclusion you have reached could work against you.

You agonize over the e-mail all weekend, and on Monday morning before the meeting your ego gets the best of you. You decide that you will resign before you are fired. You decide to give your boss a piece of your mind before you have solid information that you are indeed headed for trouble. You march into the boss's office at the appointed time with a negative attitude, not knowing that he or she is about to offer you a promotion. Before your boss has a chance to utter a word, you give him or her a piece of your mind. The boss listens quietly and then replies, "Well, it's too bad you feel this way. I actually had a good promotion for you, but given your terrible attitude and insulting comments, I have decided not to give you that job. Clean out your desk and leave now!" Well, my friend, you have really done it this time! By acting on a setup instead of a confirmed situation (the trigger), you have cost yourself prestige, reputation, money, and pleasure. You acted too soon. You pulled the trigger in the absence of confirmation, and you have paid for your error.

Action must follow a logical sequence. The logical sequence of events that leads to action is first the setup, or the situation that creates the POSSIBILITY of an event. Second is the trigger that tells you the event is likely to happen and will lead to the follow-through or the action. Never act without a trigger or confirmation.

Example 2: The Hunter and the Hunted

Hundreds or even thousands of hunters are injured or worse every year during hunting season, because many hunters are trigger-happy. They will shoot at anything that moves. As long as it's the color of a bear or a deer, they'll shoot at it. Hunters have been known to shoot at large brown dogs, human beings dressed in brown, human beings wearing fur coats, decorative animals in front yards and backyards, automobiles that may look like an animal from a great distance, and so on. This is another simple case of action prior to confirmation. The movement of an object is their setup. They shoot before they have confirmed that the movement is that of their prey. It's a simple case of failure to confirm that the setup should trigger action. And in the case of the hunter, failure to confirm results can be devastating.

Example 3: Rumors and Realities

Your brother-in-law calls you with a hot stock tip. He knows the son of a high-ranking corporate officer in an electronics firm that is about to announce a new discovery in the communications field. This revolutionary antenna will supposedly increase the range of any handheld communications device by 50 percent. And, the cost of adding this new device to existing communications equipment is very low. The company estimates that it can sell over 30 million units at $29 per unit in their first year of operation. What's more, a major manufacturer of communications equipment has expressed interest in buying the company.

Your brother-in-law tells you that the stock of this small company is selling at $3 per share, but that when news of its discovery becomes public the stock will soar to over $40 per share in a matter of weeks, if not days. He has already positioned himself with 5,000 shares. If the stock goes to $40, as he expects it will, his $15,000 investment will be worth $200,000.

Naturally, you're excited by the prospects of such a move, and you buy the stock. Then you hear that the news is false or exaggerated, the stock declines, and you either take your losses or you keep the stock indefinitely, expecting it will eventually go up. At some point, you may even be tempted to buy more if the rumors persist. You have hope and greed rather than reality and good sense.

Where did you go wrong? You allowed a setup to prompt you into action in the absence of confirmation. What would you need by way of confirmation? In this case, there could have been many things. You could have done your own research to confirm or negate the rumors. You could have studied the finances of the company. You could have asked more questions. You could have done a thorough search on the Internet for more information. You could have looked into the backgrounds of the officers and technical experts at the company. You could have asked your brother-in-law how successful his tips have been in the past. You could have studied the stock charts and indicators. You could even have looked into whether insider-buying activity had been going on in that stock. But you didn't do any of these and instead acted without a trigger—and you paid for it.

THE STF IN DETAIL

Hopefully, these three examples have prepared you for what I am about to formalize. But why formalize this process? The answer is simple. *Without a formal set of procedures that control the decision-making process, you will be like every other aspiring investor, a ship at sea without a captain or a course.* By following the GIM and the STF methods, you'll have won more than 75 percent of the battle for investment success.

Now let's examine the STF in detail. The STF model I would like you to visualize and memorize is shown in Figure 6.3.

If you take the time to study this model and apply it to every investment decision you make, it will serve you well. Now let's take a look at a few real-life examples of how the STF model translates into investment action and success.

STF and Gold

For many years, the price of gold moved lower. As the chart in Figure 6.4 shows, the price of gold reached a major peak in

---

FIGURE 6.3   The STF Model

Setup	Trigger	Follow-Through
Any investment opportunity based on a recommendation, research, a tip, an analysis, a newspaper article, news, rumor, historical patterns, chart analyses, computer signals, etc.	Any indication or confirmation that validates the setup as a realistic possibility. The trigger can be news, additional research, computer signals, and chart patterns.	ACTION BY THE INVESTOR

FIGURE 6.4   The Price of Gold, 1984–2003

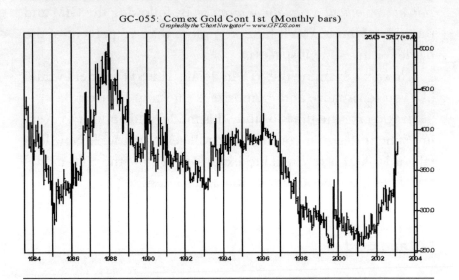

GC-055: Comex Gold Cont 1st (Monthly bars)
Graphed by the 'Chart Navigator' – www.GFDS.com

late 1987 and moved lower until mid-2000, when it started to climb again. All the way down, investors who were hopeful of a turn-around and expected international conflict and turmoil to turn prices higher bought gold *without* a trigger. In other words, they bought gold merely because the market was set up to go higher. However, it failed to trigger action and declined.

In early 2002, however, the market finally gave indications of its intention to go higher. The indications I am referring to happened on several fronts. Students of the gold market and of chart patterns (which is called technical market analysis) saw the triggers and took action accordingly. Figure 6.5 shows one of these triggers in chart form.

FIGURE 6.5   Gold triggers an up move by penetrating the "resistance level."

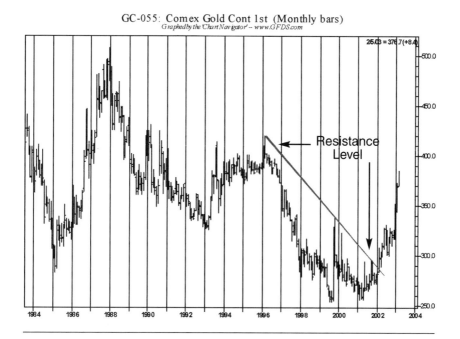

GC-055: Comex Gold Cont 1st (Monthly bars)
Graphed by the 'ChartNavigator' – www.GFDS.com

SUMMARY

Now that I have shown you the GIM and STF and explained some of the details, there are a few more issues that need to be addressed. The following questions and issues are probably on your mind. Rest assured they will be answered. For now, I ask your patience and commitment.

- How can I begin with only a few hundred dollars?

- How can I get the money to begin investing, if I don't have it yet?

- How do I know if I'm trying to move ahead too quickly?

- How do I know if I'm moving too slowly?

- Should I try to have opinions or just follow rules?

- Are opinions worthwhile or just potentially problematic?

- Should I try to do this alone or with a partner?

- What, if any, are the dangers of working alone?

- What, if any, are the dangers of working with a partner?

- Are you capable of going it alone, or are you more likely to be successful with a partner or partners?

Chapter 7 will put the model into practical application for you. Get ready, the best is yet to come.

THE METHOD

In order to put the GIM into practice, you will need a method that tells you exactly when to buy, when to sell, how much money to risk, and when to get out of an investment. The process of actually determining what and when to buy or sell is called "timing." Timing fits into the *confirmation* step of the GIM. Whether you are a long-term investor, a short-term investor, or a day trader, the timing method that will be explained in this chapter can help you on the road to success. Because timing is extremely important, the information contained in this chapter is vital to your success. Although the information presented herein may be slightly technical to you, take your time and read it carefully. In fact, study it as you would a science book. If you are having difficulty with the concepts or the charts, see the introductory book I wrote with my son Elliott, *Stock Market Strategies That Work* (McGraw-Hill, 2001).

In this chapter I will give you the tools you'll need for investment success: how to implement the GIM model and STF method with timing.

While some of you may think that this is the most important chapter in the book, I assure you that this is *not* the case. This chapter reveals no secrets, no magic potion, no instant get-rich-quick fairy dust, and no surefire success method. Instead, this chapter will expand my logical, step-by-step, no-sex-appeal method for guiding you to financial success. If you want sex appeal and secrets, watch late-night television infomercials and read your junk mail. "These wonderful secrets can be yours for only 4 payments of $49 plus shipping and handling. And if you order within the next 30 minutes you can also get the *Do-It-Yourself Instant Mega Millionaire Kit* at no additional charge. If you're not totally satisfied, you can return the entire package within 30 days for a full refund (minus shipping and handling)." No, you won't find any of that in this chapter. But you will find logic, consistency, and time-tested suggestions, which when combined with the GIM and STF methods will help you along the road to success more quickly than you had hoped or expected.

SELECTION AND TIMING OF INVESTMENTS

This seemingly simple topic has been the subject of thousands of books, hundreds of seminars, and thousands of articles. You can't buy a copy of *Forbes* magazine or any of the numerous other financial publications without being exposed to recommendations and suggestions. I'm sure you've seen the provocative headlines . . .

- Ten Stocks to Buy Now for Your Retirement Years

- Stocks That Can Double Next Year

- Riding the Profit Wave of Biotechnology

- Gold Stocks for the Small Investor

- The Power of Options Trading

- High Income Stocks for the Higher Risk Investor

- Properties to Buy Now for Tomorrow's Big Profits

The sad fact about most, if not all, of these alluring head-lines is that they are designed mainly to entice you to buy the publication. If you examine the recommendations in retrospect, you'll find that many of them failed to pan out. What's worse, in many cases the recommendations went bad before they turned to the good. And while the individuals who recommended these strategies or investments can come back in one year and state that their strategies made money, they fail to tell you what happened in the interim. For example, if a stock was recommended as a buy at $30 per share and it declined to $10 per share thereafter, many investors would have bailed out, taking the loss. If the stock thereafter went up to $44 per share, the individuals who recommended the stock can state that they were correct in their forecast. In the long run, the recommendation made money IF you did not panic and sell when the stock declined and IF you had the patience and emotional strength to hold on and IF you didn't get out at the first sign of recovery in the price of the stock. Skillful financial writers, analysts, or stock pickers can pull the wool over your eyes and look good when they are, in fact, wrong. There are only a handful of market timers out there in the investment world who have been consistently good at their job. (I name names in the Resources at the back of the book, but don't go there yet!) I want you to be your own expert and your own stock picker. I want you to become independent.

Remember that there are basically five types of experts in the investment field. They are as follows:

1. *The biased expert.* Forget about these people! They usually work for brokerage houses. Because of the stock-picking scandals that surfaced in the early 2000s and changes implemented to avoid such problems in the future, many brokerage houses have separated their research departments from their sales departments. Many independent research firms have come forward as alternatives. This may prove helpful. However, I strongly advise you to avoid any brokerage house research and recommendations, because they will likely be biased sooner or later.

2. *The general trend follower.* These individuals are good at analyzing and forecasting the general direction of markets. They can correctly forecast pig-picture trends—the direction stocks are likely to move over the next three to five years and the outlook for the real estate market. Such information can be helpful but in some cases is not specific enough. However, the work of some good general trend followers out there is worth following.

3. *The marker timer.* These individuals have a shorter-term focus than the general trend follower. They want to pick market turns that are shorter term in nature and seek to move in and out with the twists and turns in stock trends. There are several excellent market timers but they are subject to some of the limitations we will discuss later on.

4. *The stock picker.* There are thousands of stock pickers who claim to have excellent records. In most cases, their work is less than 50 percent accurate. They make their money by getting out of losing positions quickly, while riding winning positions for a longer time. Following a stock picker has its good points and its bad points. The good points are you don't have to do the work yourself and they're good at what they do. The bad news is they have their downtimes as well as uptimes and you'll have to pay for their services. Finally, some stock pickers and market timers are better in some areas than in others. Some are especially good at mutual fund timing, whereas others are excellent gold stock pickers. If you want to have a balanced list of investments, you may need to follow a group of experts and deal with opinions that are, at times, contradictory.

5. *The sector expert.* These people excel in one area or another. They are highly focused, tend to have tunnel vision, and are all too often fanatical in their points of view. You will find many of the "gold bugs" in this camp. The good news is they usually know their stuff. The bad news is they will often stick to their expectations through thick and thin and all too often their timing is bad. They may continue to recommend a given strategy, even if it has been a losing one for many years. Eventually, they will be right and they'll never let you forget it! Don't get me wrong. There are some excellent names in this area but don't go here with the intention of putting all your eggs in one basket. Diversification is the name of the investment game!

INTRODUCING THE METHOD

It is difficult to write an investment guide that will be tailored to the level of expertise of all investors. Some of you may be completely new to the stock market, while others will have had many years of experience. If I begin at too basic a level, I run the risk of alienating those with more experience. If I begin at too advanced a level, I'll lose the beginner. Accordingly, please find your place in the following list and act accordingly:

- *Complete newcomers to investing.* If you have had no experience in the stock market, you need to learn the basic terminology of the market. If you have no experience in real estate, you'll need a working knowledge in this area as well. I suggest reading *Stock Market Strategies That Work*. It will help you become acquainted with the basics and with many of the important issues. There are other books for beginners that may be more basic. It may take a little more time for you to get started, but I urge you to build a sound base of knowledge before you invest a single penny in stocks.

- *You have had some experience but . . .* This category is one step above being a newcomer, but it's an important step because you have learned some of the basics. Here again, I recommend my book *Stock Market Strategies That Work*.

- *You're an experienced investor.* This means you have traded in stocks, options, futures, or all of these. You have a good understanding of the terminology used in stock investing and trading. I suggest that you read my books, *Momentum Stock Selection* (McGraw-Hill, 2001) and *How to Trade the New Single Stock Futures* (Dearborn Trade, 2002). These books will help you with the concepts discussed in this chapter.

As an alternative, you may want go ahead with this chapter, regardless of your experience level. If things don't make sense to you, then go back to the basics and read the recommended books. Note that there are many books for beginners, so choose one that you enjoy or that is more on your level of knowledge and experience. Now let's proceed with the topic at hand.

Many Different Methods

There are literally thousands of investment and trading methods in the stock, options, and futures markets. Truth be known, most of them are only marginally successful for various and sundry reasons. If you can find a method that has been profitable 50 percent of the time, and if you manage your losing investments by exiting them quickly while you keep winning investments, you will do well in the long run. Few professional investors are correct a majority of the time. Too many investors are preoccupied with the question, What percentage of the time has your investment decision been correct? The question is not only a foolish one, but it can also get you into trouble. The important question is not how often has a system or methodology been right, but rather how much money has an investment method made for individuals at your financial level.

Consider the following scenarios:

- Investor #1: Ten investments at 90 percent correct. One investment lost money, the others made money.

- Investor #2: Ten investments at 30 percent correct. Seven investments lost money, only three made money.

Which of these two is best? Most people would pick the investor #1 approach, but the choice would be impossible to make without more information. Consider the following:

- Investor #1: Ten investments at 90 percent correct. One investment lost $2,000, the others made a total of $457 after commissions. Net LOSS: $1,543.

- Investor #2: Ten investments at 30 percent correct. Seven investments lost a total of $2,500. Three investments made a total of $5,000. Net PROFIT: $2,500.

Which of these two is best? Clearly the second choice is the correct one. Note that for investor #1, accuracy was excellent but the results were poor.

Investment Methods, Accuracy, and Risk

As you can see from the foregoing example, accuracy is not the issue. If you have a method that is both accurate and profitable, you have the best combination. Although this chapter is about an investment method, I will tell you frankly that if you manage your risk correctly, then virtually any method can make you money if you follow some basic rules. These rules are discussed at the end of this chapter. I believe that the methods discussed in this book can boost your accuracy well over the 60 percent level. This advantage, combined with effective risk management, can give you excellent and consistent results for many years.

INTRODUCING MOMENTUM

There are many ways to measure the strength or weakness of a stock. There are many ways in which we can attempt to determine if a stock is ready to go up or down. Momentum is one of the many technical methods used to measure the strength or weakness of a stock. I will use the abbreviation MOM for momentum. I like to think of MOM as a measure of underlying market strength or weakness and of change in direction (or trend). In fact, I like the analogy of fuel in a gas tank. If a stock is going to continue to move higher, it must have sufficient fuel, or momentum, to do so. If a stock or futures contract is going to continue going down, it must have sufficient fuel, or momentum, to push it lower. If a market is moving higher, while its momentum, as measured by the MOM indicator, is moving lower, the market is in danger of topping. If a market is moving lower, while its MOM indicator is moving higher, then the market is developing a bottoming pattern.

Each of these conditions is defined as a *divergent* condition. *Divergence* means moving in different directions. Markets that are likely to change direction tend to develop divergence before they change direction. *Divergence does not always happen prior to a change in the direction of a market, but it often does.* Why is this important? Because if you are going to make money on your investments, you will want to buy when markets are either low in price or likely to go up. And you will want to get out before markets go down, or soon after they begin going down. You will take your profits and put them into other investments using this approach.

The Normal Situation

First, let's take a look at the "normal" conditions for price and momentum. Figure 7.1 shows a normal uptrend (bull trend) in which momentum and price are moving up together. This is a "healthy" market, one in which a top is not likely at this time. Figure 7.2 shows a declining trend (bear trend) in which price and momentum are declining. This is also a "normal" pattern in which the odds of a continued drop in price are quite good.

FIGURE 7.1   This illustration shows momentum with price. Note that as price moves higher, momentum moves higher. The "vehicle" has fuel behind it and, as a result, a top is not imminent. Of course, this *can change* quickly, depending on the behavior of the MOM indicator.

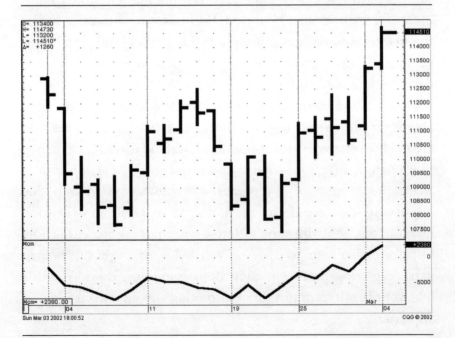

FIGURE 7.2 The relationship between momentum and price as price declines. As price moves down, momentum becomes more negative, suggesting that there is still power behind the declining trend.

HOW TO CALCULATE MOMENTUM

Don't let this scare you; MOM is simple to calculate. You do not need to know how to calculate momentum, but if you want to know, remember that it involves simple subtraction. In order to get the MOM indicator, you simply subtract one day's closing price from the closing price *X* days ago. Here are a couple examples:

1. *Ten-day momentum calculation for stock ABC.* Price today: 64.10. Price ten days ago: 64.50. Momentum = 64.50 − 64.10, or −0.40. The momentum is NEGATIVE, because the price today was lower today than ten days ago.

2. *Ten-day momentum calculation for stock XYZ.* Price today: 2.22. Price ten days ago: 2.18. Momentum = 2.22 − 2.18, or +4.0. The momentum is POSITIVE, because the price today was higher than ten days ago. Momentum is zero if the price today is the same as it was *X* days ago.

Some trading software and charting programs use the Rate of Change (ROC) instead of the MOM. The calculation for ROC involves dividing one number by another rather than subtracting. In terms of the shape of the momentum indictor when plotted on a chart, however, the end result is the same. As I said before, don't let this discussion scare you. You will not need to know how to calculate MOM, unless you do not have access to the Internet. If you have access to the Internet, either through your own computer or an Internet facility, you can get the MOM online, usually at no charge.

WHAT DOES MOMENTUM TELL US ABOUT A MARKET?

I consider momentum to be a "fuel gauge indicator" for the markets. Whether we use MOM for stocks or futures, it tells us how much available energy a market has:

- When a market is moving higher, momentum should be moving higher.

- When a market is moving lower, momentum should be moving lower.

These two conditions are normal conditions for a market. When conditions become abnormal or divergent, that should alert us to possible changes in market trends.

DIVERGENCE AND CHANGES IN TREND

There are two conditions that can signal a pending change in the trend of a market. They are as follows:

1. Bearish Divergence—PENDING MARKET TOP. This condition is signaled by price moving HIGHER, while momentum is moving LOWER.

2. Bullish Divergence—PENDING MARKET BOTTOM. This condition is signaled by price moving LOWER, while momentum is moving HIGHER.

These conditions can be readily observed if you plot momentum on a price chart. The time length for MOM we will use is 28 periods. This length was determined through my study and analysis of the markets. Take a few minutes to examine the illustrations in Figures 7.3 and 7.4, which show the positive and negative divergence conditions. By 28 periods I mean 28 days or 28 weeks. The long-term approach I am recommending in this book is based on weekly prices. Therefore, the momentum we will use is 28 weeks in length. In other words, the price at the end of this week subtracted from the ending price 28 weeks ago.

I want to stress a few points before going on. Let's go back to the GIM. Remember that the GIM consists of five steps. Here is how these steps "work" in relation to the MOM timing method:

1. *Historical pattern.* The historical pattern that leads us to expect a particular move in a stock is based on the theory and observed history of momentum and price (as explained in this chapter). The pattern is simple: A price higher with MOM lower is a negative pattern (i.e., a sell pattern); a price lower with MOM higher is a positive pattern (i.e.,

a buy pattern). The existence of a pattern does not lead to action; it merely leads to an expectation.

2. *Expectation.* We anticipate that a stock will go up or down based on the history of the pattern and its current configuration. An expectation is nothing more than an expectation. It is NOT a call to action. If you act on an expectation, you are not following the method.

3. *Confirmation.* Confirmation in this case comes when the MOM indicator has given a signal to buy or sell as discussed in this chapter. The buy or sell confirmation is specific and 100 percent objective. There is no interpretation, no deliberation, no analysis, and no deep thinking. The switch is either on or off.

4. *Action.* Action is necessitated by confirmation. In this case, the action you take will be to buy or sell.

5. *Management.* Once you have taken action, you will follow through with effective management of risk in order to maximize your profits and minimize your losses.

Examples of Bearish (Down) and Bullish (Up) Divergence

Figure 7.3 shows bullish divergence. You will note that as the price of this market moves lower, the momentum continues to move higher. To me this means that the market is being "accumulated" by traders who may either know or think they know something bullish. In any event, the rising momentum with the declining price SETS UP a possible low. Note that this configuration *does not tell you to buy immediately.* It only sets up a potential low.

FIGURE 7.3 Bullish Divergence. Note how momentum continued higher, while the price of the market continued lower into late January. As the price was moving lower, momentum was moving higher.

Figure 7.4 shows bearish divergence. Note that as the price of this market moves higher, the momentum continues to move lower. To me this means that the market is being sold by traders who may either know something bearish or think they know something bearish. In any event, the falling momentum with the rising price SETS UP a possible top. Note that this configuration *does not tell you to sell immediately.* It only sets up a potential top.

The bullish divergence preceded an explosive rally in this market. Take a few minutes to study the chart in Figure 7.3. It is a classic example of how a change in the direction of momentum precedes the start of a new bullish trend.

FIGURE 7.4 Bearish Divergence. Note how momentum continued lower, while the price of the market continued higher. The stock dropped substantially after the bearish divergence pattern.

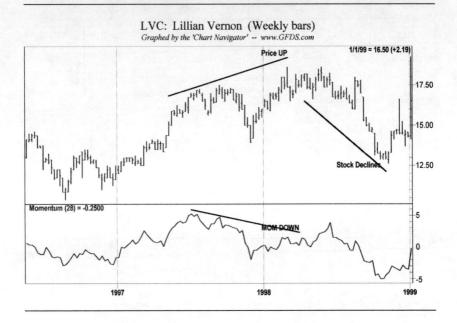

It is important to remember that the illustration in Figure 7.3 *does not,* in and of itself, tell us WHEN to buy. It only tells us that a change in the trend is likely. Sometimes the change will develop whereas on other occasions bullish divergence fails to develop into an actual signal to buy.

Let's go back for a few minutes to our STF discussion. If you recall, I advised you to think of investments as having three parts, the Setup, the Trigger, and the Follow-Through. The process of finding stocks that have momentum divergence is the process of finding setups. The setup itself *does not* trigger an investment. Please read this carefully and understand it. It will make you money and, above all, SAVE you money and prevent you from making blunders!

This is why we need to use another aspect of the MOM to actually get us into specific stocks as investments. This topic will be discussed next. First, however, let's take a look at how bearish divergence precedes market tops. See Figure 7.4.

Bearish divergence preceded a strong decline in this market. Take a few minutes to study this chart. It is a classic example of how a change in the direction of momentum precedes the start of a new bearish trend.

It is important to remember that the illustration in Figure 7.4 *does not,* in and of itself, tell us WHEN to sell. It only tells us that a change in the trend is likely. Sometimes the change will develop, whereas on other occasions bearish divergence will fail to develop into an actual signal to sell.

This is why we need to use another aspect of momentum to actually get us into the markets.

TIMING, TIMING, TIMING

Timing is the critical element that investors and traders have failed to understand correctly when using momentum. As I have stated above, the mere fact that divergence is developing does not mean that it's time to buy or sell. YOU MUST WAIT FOR A SIGNAL. The MOM timing signal is very specific. Here's how it works:

- *Buy signal.* Once a period of bullish divergence has developed for six time frames (i.e., days if you are using daily charts, weeks if you are using weekly charts), then you BUY when momentum exceeds the highest level it has attained during the period of bullish divergence. This condition is shown in chart form in Figure 7.5.

FIGURE 7.5　The price of this market made a new low at point A. The new low at point A was *not* accompanied by a new low in momentum at point B. As you can see, momentum B is higher than momentum C, while price low A is lower than price low D. This establishes the period of bullish divergence. Point E is the highest momentum point between momentum points C and B. The penetration of point E at point X yields the momentum *buy* signal prior to a substantial rally.

- *Sell signal.* Once a period of bearish divergence has developed for six time frames (i.e., days if you are using daily charts, weeks if you are using weekly charts), then you SELL when momentum declines below the lowest level it has attained during the period of bearish divergence. This condition is shown in chart form in Figure 7.6.

Figure 7.6 shows the opposite situation. It shows how a top forms on bearish divergence and the sell signal trigger based in penetration of point E, which is the momentum sell point.

FIGURE 7.6 The price of this market made a new high at point A. The new high at point A was *not* accompanied by a new high in momentum at point B. As you can see, momentum B is lower than momentum C, while price high A is higher than price high D. This establishes the period of bearish divergence. Point E is the lowest momentum point between momentum points C and B. The penetration of point E at point X yields the momentum *sell* signal prior to a substantial decline.

That's it. It's simple, but it will take you a while to learn how to spot the divergence and the signals. I do believe that after you've done this for a while, you'll get the hang of it and you'll be able to jump on board big moves, either before they happen or just as they're beginning to happen. Although the momentum method is not infallible, I believe it can alert you to major moves, either before they begin or in the very early stages of their development. The momentum method can work in a different time frame as well. If you're a short-term or day trader, you'll want to use intraday charts in order to get the signals correctly for these time frames.

WHERE DO I GET THE MOM?

Now that you know the method, you will need to practice it. But practice requires you to have access to MOM charts. There are several choices:

- *Keep your own charts and calculate MOM on your own.* This is labor-intensive and truly a waste of time, because you can get the MOM online for a small fee by subscribing to a chart service (it may be free at some Web sites).

- *Subscribe to a charting service that will allow you to get a chart on virtually any market with the MOM indicator on it.* These services vary in price from about $40 monthly on the low end to as much as $700 monthly on the high end. You do not need to spend high-end money to get MOM charts.

The Resources section at the end of this book gives you the names of services that are either free or fee-based for getting the MOM indicator.

PRACTICE, PRACTICE, PRACTICE!

Now that you know the MOM method and can identify divergence as well as entry signals, the key to your success will depend on several factors, the first of which is practice. You must become completely skilled at the application of the MOM method.

Manage Risk

One aspect of success, as you well know, is to manage your risk effectively. This requires the use of stop losses based either on dollar risk stops or on a technical approach. If you want more information on this aspect of the MOM method, I refer you to my book *Momentum Stock Selection* (McGraw-Hill, 2001), which is available at my online bookstore, <www.invest-store.com/ tradefutures>. This book will help you sort out the details of risk management with this important trading method.

Practice Charts

Because this method requires practice, I have included a few practice charts for you. These charts show various time frames and various markets, along with my analysis of the patterns. I cannot stress too strongly the importance of practice. Although this method is simple and easily applied, it *will* take practice. Chapter 8 will give you specifics on how you can apply the MOM method to various investment budgets.

Finally, I want you to understand this approach fully before you invest a single penny. Therefore, if you have questions on the MOM method, send me an e-mail at jake@trade-futures.com. You will get a reply as quickly as possible from either myself or an assistant, but please be patient because I get many e-mails every day.

PRACTICE CHART 1 This chart shows a developing bearish momentum divergence, because prices made a new peak but momentum was moving lower in early February as prices climbed. Eventually this market declined.

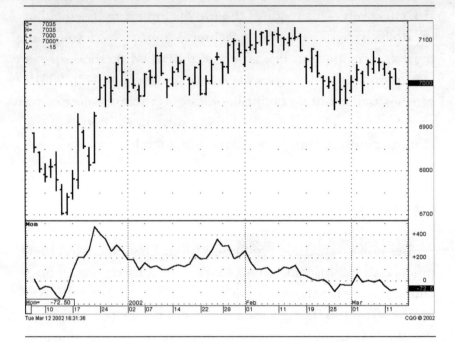

PRACTICE CHART 2 This chart shows a classical momentum divergence low pattern. Note how prices made a new low in early November, while MOM did not do so. Eventually MOM went ABOVE its high point of the divergence period, which was established in the week of 29 October. This point was penetrated in early November, after which the market moved dramatically higher.

PRACTICE CHART 3   Here is another classic example of a stock that is clearly bottoming based on bullish divergence. As you can see, the MOM is rising as prices are declining. In fact, a low was made and momentum continued to climb. This stock will enter its BUY point if and when it exceeds the highest momentum level on this chart. This level occurred at the end of the week of 12 April 2002.

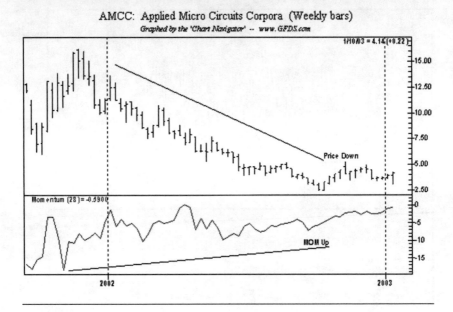

AMCC: Applied Micro Circuits Corpora (Weekly bars)
Graphed by the 'Chart Navigator' -- www.GFDS.com

PRACTICE CHART 4   Amazon.com bottomed in a classical MOM pattern. As prices moved down, MOM was moving up. When the high point of the MOM divergence period was penetrated (as shown by my buy notation), the stock began to go higher. It moved from about $14 per share to a peak of $25 per share.

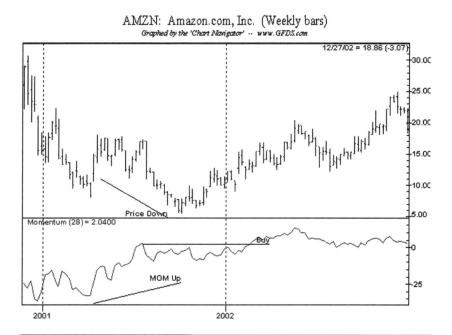

AMZN: Amazon.com, Inc. (Weekly bars)
Graphed by the 'Chart Navigator' -- www.GFDS.com

PRACTICE CHART 5   This chart shows a stock that is now bottoming. As you can see from my notes, a new low has been made in price, while MOM has been rising. The buy point has been established and we are waiting for a TRIGGER to occur.

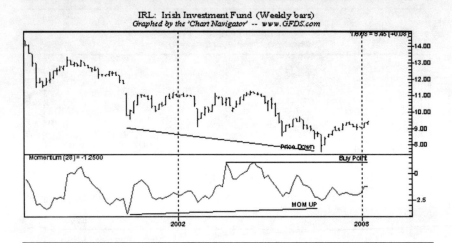

IRL: Irish Investment Fund (Weekly bars)
Graphed by the 'Chart Navigator' -- www.GFDS.com

PRACTICE CHART 6   This chart shows two situations. First, a MOM divergence sell at the far left of the chart and, as of the end of the chart, a MOM divergence buy setup. Can you find the proper points?

PRACTICE CHART 7   A sell pattern is developing. Can you find it?

Tue Mar 12 2002 16:35:25   CQG © 2002

CHAPTER EIGHT

GAMBLE OR INVEST YOUR WAY TO WEALTH?

As an investor you have many choices. You can be conservative, aggressive, long-term oriented, or short-term oriented. You can be a day trader or mutual fund investor, or you can trade the new single stock futures (SSF) market. What you decide to do depends on a number of factors, the most important of which are your financial ability, personality, self-discipline, level of experience, and available time. No matter what you decide to do, you must follow the time-tested rules of profitable investing. Although this seems like a reasonable and relatively simple thing to do, the sad fact is that most investors, even experienced ones, will not follow through consistently.

Unfortunately, too many of us give in to the gambler within us. After all, we believe erroneously, it takes much less work to be a gambler than it does to be an investor. This just isn't true! Successful gamblers have honed their skills to a virtual science. They put hours of work into their craft. And, there are good gamblers and bad gamblers, just as there are good investors and bad investors. You must decide whether you want to be an investor or a gambler. Once you have made that decision, decide whether you want to be a good gambler or a good investor as opposed to a bad gambler or a bad investor.

Because it takes just as much effort to be a good investor as it does to be a good gambler, you might as well be a good investor. However, if you decide to gamble, you don't need this book and can stop reading now. This chapter will educate you in the finer details of investing and will also give you some details on what will work and what is not likely to work for you as an investor.

Now that you have learned how to implement the GIM and STF models, let's look at several very important issues that tend to undermine our goals and success. After doing so, I will tell you about the six major investment categories that can take you to your goals—while you maintain your regular job.

Today's investment world is highly competitive and very risky. The waters are often difficult to navigate. The amount of information that can be obtained on virtually any investment is often overwhelming. The decision-making process is, for many investors, difficult and confusing. Opinions abound. Will we have inflation or deflation? Will we suffer an economic meltdown? Will the U.S. dollar be massacred in the world markets? Will there be a war, and if so, what will its effect be on the U.S. economy? Will the Social Security fund go broke? Will the price of oil go to $100 per barrel? Will the Republicans raise or lower taxes? Will more airlines go broke? What will happen to the stock market in the event of another terrorist attack on the United States? Where is my money safe? The list goes on and on.

It seems that the more you read, the more confused you get. Some experts tell us that everything will be fine. Other experts cry wolf repeatedly. Some radical thinkers want us to believe that an economic collapse will bring anarchy. They tell us to head for the hills with ammunition, guns, medical supplies, gas masks, antibiotics, and a year's supply of food. Yes, it's all very confusing. As I mentioned before, some of the experts who may have been highly regarded in the past have shown themselves to be frauds and flimflams. To make matters worse, we have been led to believe that the investment game can only be won by professionals who have an edge on the average person. After all, professionals have inside information. They have a pipeline to those in the know and connections in Washington. They have the kind of financial power that moves markets. Furthermore, they don't make mistakes, always seem to be in on the big moves, and always seem to make big money at the expense of those who are at the bottom of the investment food chain.

Adding to this bleak picture is the fact that the average person can't afford to hire an expensive financial advisor or accomplished money manager with a record of profits and consistency. More and more, investment success seems downright impossible for the average individual. In an atmosphere of frustration, we feel why even try because we won't succeed at this highly competitive game. And this, in turn, fosters the feeling that we might as well gamble rather than invest.

The gambling business has mushroomed in recent years, due in part to the frustration that has besieged the average investor. All too often, we feel that gambling is the way to go. And the incentives are many. In many states, it's only a 45-minute drive or less to a gambling spot, whether a casino in a gambling town, a riverboat casino, an offtrack betting parlor, or a lottery ticket outlet. The idea that a one dollar lotto ticket can yield $100 million or more is certainly an alluring one. And the lure of becoming a multimillionaire easily overcomes the odds for many of us. The burgeoning of lottery ticket sales reflects, in part, the financial crisis so many states have been having since the late

1980s. Although the purported reason for beginning state lotteries was to fund a cash-hungry educational system, many states merely used it as an excuse to raise revenues to cover wasteful spending, favoritism, graft, and self-serving politicians. Clearly, this also has added to the anger and frustration of investors. It's enough to make one want to give up altogether on investing.

THE INSTANT AGE

The piling on of frustrations in virtually all aspects of modern life has encouraged individuals to seek immediate gratification instead of focusing on long-range goals. The reasoning is simple and logical: Why wait until tomorrow if the world is so riddled with problems today? Our "age of instantism" may cause us to avoid investing, to spend rather than save, and to gamble rather than invest. We want it fast or faster, and we want it big and often—instant access to the Internet, faster cars, faster boats, faster planes, and higher speed limits. We want instant mashed potatoes, instant relief from pain, fast service at the drive-through, speedy hospital stays, instant pictures via our cell phones, and fast executions of stock purchases and sales. The age of instantism has also undermined and dissuaded the investor. We want success and we want it now.

CONTRADICTIONS, CONFLICTS, AND CONSISTENCY

We are torn between going for the fast buck with high risk or seeking the slow and steady path to financial success. The seeming contradictions of modern society help contribute to conflict and inconsistent behaviors. Hopefully, by the time you have finished reading this book, you will have developed a long-range view. You will have a clear sense of the big picture, while understanding the small picture. And better yet, if you are indeed still tempted by short-term profits, you will find several resources and rules by which you can satisfy this need as well. But remember, do so only after you have mastered the big picture. Don't be lured into playing the fast game without a proper foundation, or you'll see your money disappear right before your eyes.

NARROWING THE FIELD OF CHOICES

Virtually any area of investment can allow you the opportunity to make big bucks. You can make your fortune methodically, or you can try to gamble your way to wealth. There's no doubt that every investment involves a degree of risk, but there's a difference between a calculated risk and an outright gamble. Within the framework of the MOM, GIM, and STF models I have given you, let's look at some specifics.

Ten Surefire Ways to Lose Your Money

Any tool, no matter how good or how safe, can become lethal in the hands of a fool. The investment tools I have given you in this book have the power to create wealth as well as the power to take it away. Here are some things to remember if you want to avoid the traps that investors fall into, even with powerful tools like the MOM method:

- You *will* lose your money if you act impulsively *before* the setup in the STF model is triggered. *You must wait for the trigger.*

- You *will* become frustrated and lose money if you are inconsistent in the application of my rules. Patience and persistence are necessary if the method is to work for you.

- You *will* lose money if you are too anxious to exit an investment if it moves against you. Make certain that you give your investments time and flexibility to work.

- You *will* lose most of your money, sooner rather than later, if you attempt to second-guess the method or attempt to combine too many other ingredients (i.e., information) into the recipe.

- You *will* lose money if you try to take on too many shares of a stock before you have sufficient experience and capital to do so. Be conservative until you have the money and the practice to be a more aggressive investor.

- You *will* lose money if you take your profit too quickly. Remember the examples I gave in Chapter 7? One loss could wipe out all your profit from the last seven investments you made.

- You *will* lose money and time and patience if you do not exit a losing investment when the time is right. Losses tend to become worse over time if you hold on to a losing position.

- You *will* lose money if you listen to too many people. Listen only to your own good advice based on a solid method of analysis, even if it isn't the MOM I taught you in this book.

- You *will* lose money if you try to make your work too complicated by combining options and other vehicles with your investments before you know how to do it.

- You *will* lose money if you fall behind in your homework. Once you have entered an investment position, you must "baby-sit" that position until it has been closed out or exited.

The Odds of Winning versus the Odds of Losing

Regardless of the methods you are using, it's reasonable to ask about the odds of success. Here are some of my thoughts regarding this important question. As you know, investing is not a surefire, foolproof proposition. There is always a risk of loss. In fact, the odds of losing on any one investment may be greater than the odds of winning on any one investment. But that's not important in the scheme of things. What's important is the bottom line, or end result. However, the process of getting to the bottom line profitably is an important one. I would estimate that if you can follow a solid method or stock selection, such as the MOM, combining it with the principles of the GIM and STF methods I taught you earlier, your odds of making money should be over 60 percent. Remember, this estimate assumes that you have followed the rules and requirements outlined in previous chapters. I do not expect you to be perfect; however, I do remind you that your overall success is very much dependent on consistency. You can work very hard to double your money only to watch all of your profit disappear because of one mistake that could have been avoided.

The Six Major Vehicles to Financial Freedom

There are six vehicles that you can use, either individually or in combination, to take you to your goal using the MOM method described in this book. When combined with the rules of the GIM and the STF techniques, these vehicles can help you make consistent profits on your investments, even if you begin with a small amount of money. These six vehicles are:

1. *Stocks.* By stocks, I mean the good old-fashioned stock market. I am not suggesting any sophisticated strategies, options programs, or highly speculative undertakings.

2. *Stock options.* This more specialized field is also capable of being your vehicle to success; however, the game is a much more difficult one and requires considerably more expertise. Many brokers will tell you that if you have limited capital, stock options can be your best bet. I disagree. In reality, too many investors lose money with stock options, and I therefore suggest if you are a beginner that you steer clear. See the Resources at the back of the book for some information sources that might assist you in learning more about the stock options market.

3. *Mutual funds.* Mutual funds are truly a wonderful area for the small investor; however, not all mutual funds are created equal. I will discuss this in Chapters 9 and 10.

4. *Single stock futures.* This is a new area of investment, but one that is highly speculative. Instead of putting up 100 percent of your money to buy stocks, you put up 20 percent of the money. This is called leverage. It can work for you or it can work against you. If you're a new investor, I suggest steering clear of single stock futures (SSFs) until you have gained some experience. SSFs should be traded only by experienced investors. Read my book, *How to Trade the New Single Stock Futures* (Dearborn Trade, 2002).

5. and 6. *Futures and Futures options.* Futures and futures options are the single most risky investments and definitely *not* recommended for the newcomer. In fact, even experienced investors should stay away from this market, unless or until they have accumulated healthy nest eggs in their accounts. Futures trading can be a highly effective addition to a stock portfolio; however, it is risky, volatile, and only appropriate for higher-risk investors. Those who want to learn about futures trading are advised to get my book, *Profit in the Futures Markets!* (Bloomberg Press, 2002).

The seasoned investor may consider all of the above either individually or in combination as part of an overall investment program. But remember that when it comes to investing, learning how to "walk" before you "run" is paramount to your financial well-being. You don't want to take your hard-earned money and throw it away by playing a game that is dominated by professionals whose only goal is to take your money.

HOW THE STOCK MARKET CAN BE A GAMBLE

If you want to gamble with your money, there are many ways in which the stock market will gladly accommodate you. Just ignore the rules in this book, take tips from friends, pick stocks haphazardly, and buy and sell stocks based on your intuition, and you'll be gambling rather than investing. It's easy to be a gambler in stocks rather than an investor. But remember that competing with the experts will give you the same result you'd get by playing poker with card sharks. You'll be grist for the mill.

In short, they'll take your money, beat you up, and send you home with your tail between your legs. So don't be a fool. Don't gamble in the markets; follow solid strategies.

HOW THE STOCK MARKET CAN BE AN INVESTMENT

Conversely, the stock market can be your vehicle to success if you plan ahead and act with more intelligence than emotion. The GIM and STF rules are simple, the approach is practical, the strategy is easily implemented, it takes very little money to get started, and the results can be very favorable. Consider the fact that you can double your money every seven to ten years just by investing conservatively. By being a little more aggressive and starting with more money, you can accumulate a very large amount of money over the span of 25 to 30 years. If you're between 15 and 25, your potential to retire at an early age with a large sum of money is quite good, *if* you follow the rules.

HOW THE STOCK MARKET CAN BE USED FOR TRADING

When you have made some important inroads on your way to success, you can expand your base of operations into trading. There are many things you can do as a trader, but unless you have first mastered investing, trading may not be the thing for you. There are many different techniques you can use for trading, and there are many different types of trading. The MOM method combined with the GIM and the STF rules discussed in this book can easily be used for short-term trading and even day

trading. As I said earlier, don't go there unless you have sufficient risk capital and unless you have learned the rules of investing first.

REAL ESTATE AND
THE GENERAL INVESTMENT MODEL

Here are some of my thoughts on real estate. They may
anger some people, but I'm here to tell you what I have learned
in my 35 years or more as a trader, investor, educator, and market analyst:

- *Some of my best investments have been in real estate.* I have rarely
  lost money in residential real estate, and the homes I have
  owned have been fantastic investments. I believe that real
  estate can be a fantastic investment for anyone who has
  the patience to buy when prices are lower and hold on
  until prices rise.

- *If you plan on investing in real estate, take your time and buy in
  your comfort zone.* By this I mean buy properties in areas
  that you are familiar with. Usually, they will be close to
  where you live. You have to know the market and understand the history of the market, and the easiest way to do
  this is by investing in your own area. My best profits have
  come from buying and selling in my own neighborhood.

- *You can use the GIM and the STF models to time your entry and
  exit in the real estate market.* Real estate in the United States
  has shown a pattern of about 18.3 years from one low point
  to the next. The years 2002–2003 mark the top of the real
  estate cycle. This means that major buying opportunities

in real estate may not come until 2010. Remember that the real estate market is selective, so much depends on location and the local market.

- *In a rising real estate market, you can make good money by buying run-down residential properties, fixing them up, and selling them for a good profit rather quickly.* However, this process takes work and careful attention to expenses.

- *Although there may be money to be made in the zero-down real estate game, I believe your odds of success in this game are slim indeed.*

THE GOOD NEWS AND THE BAD NEWS IN FUTURES TRADING

The good news about futures trading is twofold: The market has excellent leverage, and there is considerable volatility. This means that you can buy and sell futures contracts for as little as 1 percent down or as much as 20 percent down in single stock futures. The bad news is that leverage and volatility also can work against you. As I stated earlier in this chapter, avoid these markets until you have some experience and success under your belt.

Fast or Slow? How to Decide

Each of the vehicles discussed in this chapter has its assets and liabilities. I have discussed these in considerable detail, so that you can decide which is best for you based on your skill, financial ability, personality, and available time. Some investors are very impatient. If they have to be in a stock for more than a few weeks to make a few hundred dollars, they are likely to be unhappy and lose their discipline. Other individuals are slow and methodical and can be in the same stocks for years and be happy. Remember the simple rule that big money is made in big moves. If you are in a stock for only a brief period of time, odds are you'll miss the big moves. But remember that you *can* be successful hitting many base hits instead of bases-loaded home runs. Only you can decide. Also, it may not be possible for you to make a decision until you have experienced other facets of investing. In so doing, you may incur losses.

In this chapter I have attempted to give you an overview of the many different vehicles you can select as your ticket to financial freedom. I have discussed the good and bad points as well as the limitations and possibilities of each approach. In closing, let me reiterate that slow is better and usually more profitable. There are many directions you can take on the road to financial freedom. Too many of them are dead ends. Although you will feel the urge to make money quickly, the consequences of attempting to do so are often devastating. If you seek to make quick profits, you must remember that the other side of the coin is quick losses. Now let's take a look at some possible investment alternatives and strategies based on your available investment capital.

STRATEGIES FOR A SHOESTRING BUDGET

The old adage "You have to have money to make money" is more true in the stock market than in virtually any other area of investing. In fact, the expression might better be stated as "The more money you have in the stock market, the more money you can make." This, of course, depends on how you handle your finances and how disciplined you are in cutting your losses short.

Most of us do not have the kind of money that allows us to invest in anything we want, at any time we want. The juxtaposition of the haves and the have-nots in American society is at times glaring. Witness the recent television documentary about popular performer Michael Jackson. The camera crew accompanied him on a Las Vegas buying spree. In ten minutes, he spent more than $1 million on vases, tables, and paintings. He nonchalantly strolled through the high-priced shop and pointed to the items he wanted. "I'll take this one and this one and this one." "Mr. Jackson, this one is $80,000," the store owner reminded him. Jackson ignored him as he continued pointing to item after item until his spending spree came to an end.

In contrast, working-class Americans struggle, often ten hours daily, to make ends meet. The vast differences in work and pay can provoke anger or it can motivate us. When we consider the fact that some actors on popular situation comedies are paid $1 million per episode, we may feel like throwing in the towel, giving up, refusing to even try to achieve such fabulous wealth. However, rather than focus on the negative, we can choose to channel our feelings in a positive and productive direction.

This chapter is written for the millions of people throughout the world who have very little to invest but who, due to their motivation and vision of the future, want to make their money work for them. They know that every lofty goal must begin with the first small step. In the 1980s, I had the good fortune to interview W. Clement Stone, the fabulously wealthy insurance tycoon, as part of a series of interviews with successful men and women for a book I was writing. I met with Mr. Stone in his private office at one of his companies, the Combined Insurance Company of America, which is located in Chicago. Stone was a dapper gentleman, dressed in an exquisite black suit, wearing his trademark bow tie. As he shook my hand firmly, I felt as though he was looking right through me. We sat and talked. "How did you become interested in business?" I asked.

He replied, "When I was 7 years old, I had a newspaper route. When I was 11 years old, I owned my own newsstand. When I was 17 years old, I started selling insurance. I walked into the biggest bank in town and asked to see the president. I introduced myself to him and asked 'May I have a moment of your time, sir?' 'Son,' he replied, 'are you here to sell me something?' 'Yes, sir, I am.' 'Then son, don't *ask* for a minute of my time, just *take* it!'"

The moral of this true little story is that you must "take the bull by the horns." Don't accept any excuses or let a lack of big money stop you. Don't allow a lack of education to limit you and don't let friends, relatives, or coworkers dissuade you or influence you with their negative attitudes. You need to begin somewhere, even if it's with the mere sum of several hundred dollars.

Yes, you *can* start with a very small amount of money, but what can you do with a few hundred bucks? This chapter examines strategies and techniques you can use to parlay your meager starting amount into a good sum. If you have more than a few hundred bucks but less than the big bucks, this chapter will also tell you how to invest larger sums.

THE THREE SHOESTRING-BUDGET STARTING LEVELS

Depending on your initial investment, I will begin by examining different plans. I will assume that the lowest starting amount for an investment plan is $500, but you *can* begin with less. Remember that the smaller your starting amount, the longer you will have to wait before you can realize good profits. As you will see, based on these starting amounts you will be adding to your account, preferably weekly from your available capital or, at the minimum, monthly.

The three levels are as follows:

1. $5,000 available starting capital

2. Less than $5,000 but more than $2,500 starting capital

3. Less than $2,500 starting capital

Although the overall strategies are similar on a smaller scale, the higher starting amount ($5,000) will allow you certain flexibilities that are not practical with smaller starting amounts. I want to stress that you *can* begin with amounts considerably less than $2,500, *but the less you begin with, the longer it will take to reach the critical mass that will facilitate more rapid profit growth.*

$5,000 AVAILABLE STARTING CAPITAL

If you begin on a shoestring budget, your choices will be significantly limited. My definition of a shoestring budget is any amount less than $5,000 as an initial investment amount. By some standards, $5,000 is a good sum of money. I don't disagree. However, in the marketplace your choices are severely limited.

One of the simplest things you can do is to begin a regular investment program in mutual funds. Mutual funds are investment companies that pool money from thousands of investors and make the decisions for you. There are many different types of mutual funds. Chapter 11 discusses some of the coming investment areas that could prove very profitable for mutual fund investors. If you invest in mutual funds, I suggest that you dollar-cost-average your investments. By this I mean simply that you buy a certain amount of the mutual fund every month or every week no matter what. In so doing, you will be forced to save, and your average cost for the mutual fund will decline if you restrict your buying only to times when the fund is lower than the average price of the shares you own.

HOW DOLLAR COST AVERAGING WORKS

The dollar cost averaging method (DCA) is a very simple but highly effective approach, particularly for the new investor or the young investor. If you would like your children to have a substantial nest egg when they get older, then DCA is the simplest and easiest way to go. You can invest the DCA way in stocks, mutual funds, or even in dividend reinvestment programs (DRIPs) as discussed later in this chapter. Your goal is to accumulate, over time, an investment position at an average price that will, eventually, be well below the price that the given stock or mutual fund is selling at today. You can use DCA in terms of price, time, or both. Here is a description of each approach.

Dollar Cost Averaging by Price

In this approach, you buy given stocks or mutual funds every time they decline to a certain price. This method is also called "scale investing" or "scale trading."

For example, you have reason to believe that the stock of the Ford Motor Company will be a good long-term investment. You reason that if Ford goes broke, the whole country is in trouble. After all, the automobile business is the backbone of the American economy. You look at a price chart for Ford and notice that since the 1970s, every time the price of Ford has been $10 or under, the stock has made a recovery and gone much higher. So you decide that $10 will be your "buy level" (BL) for Ford. You wait and watch and one day Ford drops to $10. You make your initial investment, perhaps even 100 shares (total cost not including commission is $1,000). Ford moves up thereafter to $12. You take no action. A few months later, it falls to $9 and you buy another 100 shares, at a total cost not including commission of $900. Your total investment is now $1,900 with an average cost of $9.50 per share.

The stock remains under $10 and, in fact, drops to $8.75. You have about $900 to invest, so you buy another 100 shares at $8.75. Your total cost is $875 not including commission, and you now own 300 shares. Your total investment is $1,000, plus $900, plus $875, at an average price per share of $9.25. Time passes and Ford hovers between $8.12 per share and $12 per share. The economy remains weak, and Ford can't sell as many cars as it had in a booming economy. The stock remains low for 18 months. During this period, you continue to DCA or scale-invest. Eventually, you accumulate 1,300 shares of Ford at an average cost of $8.87 per share.

Three years pass. The economy improves, and Ford shares rise to $16. Your 1,300 shares that cost you a total of $11,531 are now worth $20,800. If Ford returns to the previous price levels of good economic times, you could easily triple your investment over time.

The good news about this approach is that you will accumulate a good number of shares in quality companies at a relatively low price. The bad news is that such opportunities do not present themselves very often, and when they do, the economic outlook is often bleak, so much so that the average investor is afraid to begin an investment program. Yet, experience has shown that this is often the best time to begin investing. Furthermore, not all quality stocks will give you an opportunity to buy at such low prices. You must, therefore, have a portfolio of stocks you are monitoring for your DCA program.

What do I mean by quality stocks? The early 2000s tested virtually everyone's idea of what constitutes a quality stock. A simple rule of thumb is to select stocks that have the longest and most consistent earnings history. Among these are the 30 Dow Jones Industrial stocks and the top 25 stocks in the Standard and Poor's 500 index. I'm talking about traditional stocks like General Electric, Ford, General Motors, IBM, U.S. Steel, Archer Daniels Midland, Heinz Foods, Campbell Foods, Procter and Gamble, Pfizer, and others. The easiest way to find these stocks is to do a little investigative work, all of which can be done at no charge on the Internet or in your public library. Look for stocks that pay dividends, have paid uninterrupted dividends for many years, do not have huge debt, and have a conservative management. You'll have to do a little legwork in order to become a successful investor. The key to this approach is that it is long term and conservative.

Dollar Cost Averaging by Time

This method is also simple. In fact, it's more simple than DCA by price. First, you select your stocks or mutual funds, and then you buy a given amount every month, every three months, every six months, whatever interval you decide. You do so regardless of price, but you are far better off beginning your program when stocks are generally low; that is, when stocks have declined at least 20 percent from their most recent peaks. Another, more technical approach is to begin your program when a stock has been below its 200-day moving average for three months or longer. You can get a stock chart with a 200-day moving average online at <www.bigcharts.com> or <www.stockcharts.com>. Figure 9.1 shows a 200-day moving average for Ford.

This chart shows two time frames during which the price of Ford fell below its 200-day moving average. The line that runs close to the price is the 200-day moving average. As you can see, there were ample opportunities to begin a DCA program or to continue such a program. The investor who invested during this time frame would have considerably lowered the average cost of the investment by maintaining the DCA approach according to the rules.

As an example of how DCA investing can be highly profitable over time, consider the following hypothetical transactions based on quarterly purchases of GE. Assume that you started a monthly program when the stock fell below its 200-day moving average. As Figure 9.2 shows, you could have bought

FIGURE 9.1   The 200-Day Moving Average in Ford Motor Company

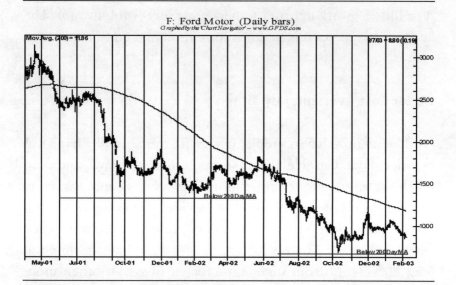

FIGURE 9.2   The 200-Day Moving Average in General Electric

shares practically every month since July 2001. Your shares would now show a loss based on your average entry price; however, this is a long-term strategy designed to give you profits over the course of several years or more. If had you started your program in July 2001, your average cost would be about $31 per share. If and when GE increases in price to $31 per share, you are even on your investment, with any price over $31 per share being profitable. Presumably, if you had been consistent with your program, you would own a large number of shares at a low average price.

DRIP YOUR WAY TO SUCCESS

DRIPs, or dividend reinvestment programs, offer a most fantastic opportunity to new investors. DRIPs are programs that allow investors to buy shares in major U.S. companies without paying commissions. If you have ever seen how much of your account goes to pay commissions, I know you'll be interested in DRIPs. To learn more about DRIPs, see the Resources at the back of the book or read about DRIPs on the Internet. There is a wealth of material available. Furthermore, there are mutual funds that invest only in DRIPs. This is an ideal situation for the smaller investor, and I highly recommend it not only from the standpoint of the DCA methods described previously, but also for the smaller investor who cannot afford a DCA approach.

LESS THAN $2,500 AVAILABLE
STARTING CAPITAL

You *can* begin with a small amount, but the investor with $500 or less is clearly at a disadvantage. Here is what I suggest:

- Begin a program of investing regularly in mutual funds.

- Consider a DCA approach in lower-priced quality stocks.

- Use DRIPs or DRIP mutual funds as your vehicle of choice. Add to your investments every month, even if only with a small amount of money. Select the mutual funds using the MOM method described in Chapter 7 or use the DCA approach explained previously. If you do not want to invest in mutual funds because they move too slowly for you, then you can invest in individual stocks.

- If you invest in individual stocks, make your selections based on the MOM method I taught you or use the DCA approach.

- If you begin with $500 or less, try to restrict your buying to stocks under $5 per share, so that you can trade 100 shares at a time. Trading in less than 100 shares at a time will cost you more in commissions, eating into your profits.

- Parlay your profits. By this I mean invest your profits by buying more shares.

- If you buy mutual funds, choose the automatic reinvestment plan for your dividends.

As you can see, you will need to begin at a relatively slow pace if you have a small amount of capital. The idea is simple. Think of it the same way you would money in a savings account. At current interest rates, money in the bank will not grow rapidly. In fact, by the time you factor in even the low rate of inflation, you are likely just marking time and not getting ahead. Therefore, it's to your advantage to put your money in a more promising "bank," the stock market. Investing on a shoestring budget can be fun as well as challenging, but you must remember a few important caveats:

- As a small investor, you do not have the money to make risky investments based on tips or rumors. Avoid these at all costs or you will see your small amount of money disappear rather quickly.

- Invest only in well-established companies that have had a lengthy history of paying dividends and whose debt is low.

- Avoid high-flying stocks that may have a great deal of promise or "sex appeal" but that do not meet the qualifications listed in the first two points.

- If and when you get dividends from your investments, put them back into your investing account.

- Do not be tempted by e-mail or postal solicitations to invest in new stock issues or in stocks that do not meet the requirements outlined here.

- If and when your total investment portfolio has doubled, you can expand your investments to include more risky stocks and perhaps ventures outside the stock market—but do so with caution.

- If and when you have doubled your investment, use a stop loss procedure to lock in at least 70 percent of the profit you have made. (Stop loss procedures are discussed in my book *Stock Market Strategies That Work*, as well as in other books on investing.)

- A wealth of free information is available via the Internet. You should not have to pay for any of the information you need in order to follow the procedures outlined in this chapter.

- Remember that the approach I have suggested here is a conservative approach. You will need to take baby steps at first.

A FEW PORTFOLIO SUGGESTIONS
FOR BEGINNERS AND SMALL INVESTORS

Here are a few suggestions for the three different levels of starting capital discussed in this chapter:

1. *$5,000 up to $20,000.* If your initial capital is over $5,000 but less than $20,000, you can follow the DCA approach as well as the momentum approaches discussed previously. Invest in the core conservative stocks that make up the 30 Dow Jones stocks, mutual funds, and only a few higher risk stocks, such as those in the biotechnology field. Do not get involved in things such as futures, single stock futures, futures options, or stock options. Do not day trade or short-term trade. For amounts over $20,000, you can be more aggressive. Look into single stock futures, covered options programs, LEAPS (long-term stock options), and even a small amount of futures trading. You can even explore some day trading in stocks. Read more books about technical analysis and higher risk investing.

2. *$2,500 to $5,000.* Stick to conservative stocks, use the DCA methods, do not use the momentum method until you have more than $10,000, and use the DCA method in mutual funds.

3. *Less than $2,500.* Be very conservative. Begin with DRIPs and other mutual funds. You can invest in a few individual stocks. Reinvest your profits. Add regularly to your investment account even if the amounts are small. You can buy mutual funds in very small dollar increments.

Finally, for all levels, I suggest that you avoid investing in "load" mutual funds. These are mutual funds that charge a fee for investing. There are many "no-load" funds that will do well for you. You can find mutual funds on line at zacks.com or morningstar.com. Attempt to buy only mutual funds that have a four-star rating or higher. You can use the DCA moving average and/or momentum methods with mutual funds in order to time your entry.

You can expand your base of operations when you have profits to show for your efforts. This will, of course, depend on how much money you have to start with and how much you can invest monthly. As a general rule, I suggest moving to a higher level of risk when you double your money or your available investment capital increases by at least 35 percent.

In closing, I want to emphasize that investing is a dynamic process. Conditions in the investment markets are constantly changing in the marketplace, and you must be adaptable. You can make money if you buy low and get out when the markets are high, or you can buy while prices are rising and get out when they have risen sharply. Either way is acceptable. The keys to successful investing are consistency, self-discipline, a long-term perspective, and knowing when to get out. I have not given too much attention to exit timing because stocks can, at times, exceed your most ambitious expectations. To set a price or a time target would not be a good thing. Therefore, my rule for exit is simple: Continue to lock in a percentage of your profit as prices move in your favor. Allow the market some leeway. Lock in 70 percent of your profits, and if you close out your investments because your stocks or mutual funds have retraced their gains, then begin your program again with your expanded base of capital.

CHAPTER TEN

GETTING SERIOUS
Strategies Beyond the Shoestring Budget

Now it gets interesting. Once you've graduated beyond the shoestring budget, or if you already have enough to begin at this level, the odds of making your money grow more rapidly are much better than if you had started with less than $5,000.

FROM $5,000 TO $20,000

As I indicated in Chapter 9, there are a number of things you can do immediately with from $5,000 to $20,000. Here are some specific suggestions, all of which can be explored in detail if you have an interest:

- *Expand into the new single stock futures market.* This market offers many opportunities for investors who are more aggressive. But before you do this, make certain that you understand the futures market. The major difference between stocks and single stock futures is that you will be investing 20 percent of the amount of your purchase. For example, if you buy 100 shares of a $20 stock, it will cost you $2,000. If you have a margin account with your broker, it will cost you $1,000, and $1,000 will be borrowed from your broker. You will pay interest on the amount you borrowed. In single stock futures, you will pay 20 percent of the total value and no interest charge. This is a more risky procedure, and you will need to know about futures and the specifics of single stock futures. I highly recommend two of my books as a prerequisite to expanding into this area: *Profit in the Futures Markets* (Bloomberg Press, 2002) and *How to Trade the New Single Stock Futures* (Dearborn Trade, 2003).

- *Another area you may want to look into is covered option writing in stocks.* There is considerable information available on this procedure, and most brokerage houses have well-run programs for this approach.

- *Begin to investigate short-term trading using technical analysis in stocks.* There are many books you can read in this area to learn the best procedures. Among these I recommend my book, *Momentum Stock Selection* (McGraw-Hill, 2001).

- *Expand your base of mutual fund investing to include more aggressive funds such as those that invest in foreign stocks, technology, and biotechnology.*

MORE THAN $10,000 BUT LESS THAN $25,000

Now we're entering the serious stage. At this level, you can consider all of the areas recommended in the previous section;

however, you also can consider the futures markets, day trading in stocks (if you have the time), or stock options trading.

MORE THAN $25,000 BUT LESS THAN $50,000

Consider all of the areas outlined above and add futures to your portfolio. Studies have shown that a balanced portfolio including stocks and futures performs better than a portfolio consisting of stocks exclusively. Do not put more than 15 percent of your funds into traditional futures trading, and do not put more than 20 percent of your funds into single stock futures or outright stock options (as opposed to covered options programs). As before, there are many excellent educational resources you can consult to expand your base of knowledge in these areas.

MORE THAN $50,000

This level, once attained, requires more attention and more serious input, including that of a financial advisor. I have previously recommended that you either hire a financial advisor or become your own financial advisor. The key is to be conservative with 70 percent of your investments and more aggressive with the remaining 30 percent. Keep your eye on the long term and expand into real estate, coins, art, and other collectibles. You may also venture into other areas such as franchises.

INVESTING IN PRECIOUS METALS AND COINS

Some of you may want to invest in coins or precious metals once you have reached the $25,000 level or higher. Investing in precious metals and/or coins is a special procedure to help protect your money in times of inflation or economic stress. Investing in these markets is not the panacea some people would have you believe. It is merely a protective strategy designed to keep your profits from deteriorating. I highly recommend the five-part investment strategy I outlined in my books, *Beat the Millennium Crash* (New York Institute of Finance, 1999) or *Investing in Metals* (Wiley, 1998).

If you have decided to expand into metals, consider the following advice:

- *Understand the general aspects of each of the metals markets.* My main task here is to provide you with a working knowledge about the basics of each major metals market. Although such information is generally known to many investors, there are important facts about the metals that are not generally known. These will assist you in planning your protective portfolio.

- *Learn if, how, and when to invest in each market.* Although some metals are ideal investment vehicles, others are not, because they are not in short supply or heavy demand. Still other metals prices are tightly controlled by a small group of producers or suppliers. These metals may or may not be suitable for investors. And still other metals may never be liquid enough to be suitable for any investor at any time. Not only will you need to know which markets to buy, but also how to buy them and how they react during periods of extreme volatility and emotion.

- *Learn about the various investment vehicles available to you, including stocks, futures, options, coins, mutual funds, and others.* Although you may know a little about each of these areas, you may wish to know more, and in particular you may want to know when each of these choices is best for you. Clearly, you will want to have some degree of diversification when an economic crisis develops. This information will help you develop a balanced portfolio of holdings.

■ *Help plan a strategy for future moves in the metals markets.* Although this book will answer many questions, it cannot possibly answer all of them. There are numerous sources to which you can turn for assistance, some of which are in book form. Still other questions can be answered by your investment advisor, financial planner, broker, or tax consultant. But remember that opinions about the direction or expected direction of the metals markets are only opinions. If you have understood what I have explained in this book, and if you share my concerns, then you will have a very good idea of how to protect yourself from what, I feel, is inevitable.

Any opinion stands a good chance of being right. If you have done your homework, if you have done your research, and if you have studied hard to anticipate the direction of the next major market shift, then do not allow your opinion to be swayed by others. Although it may be reasonable to solicit input regarding how much money to commit, how much risk you can take, or what the tax consequences of your investments might be, you might want to ignore advice about the anticipated direction of the markets. Someone else's knowledge and studies may not be as intense or as complete as yours. Don't forget to use the STF and GIM methods.

Finally, remember that investing in metals is, as I have stated previously, a highly emotional thing. The psychology of investing is a field unto itself. (I have two books on this subject to which I will refer at various points.) And though you may have done a thorough job of researching and preparing your plan, you may fail if you lack the discipline to implement your program thoroughly, consistently, and without the fear or greed that are often the undoing of otherwise successful programs. Keep your emotions in check and be aware of your motivation for taking specific actions at given times.

Although I have attempted to provide as much pertinent information as possible about each of the metals, I realize that conditions are changing rapidly in our modem world. Technology is growing at an exponential pace, and with it, new applications for metals are found virtually every day. For example, researchers recently introduced a powerful new drug for cancer treatment that uses platinum as its base. While the use of certain metals is declining, applications for other metals are on the rise. By the time you read this book, some of my comments may be out-of-date; however, the core elements presented here will likely never be out-of-date. As long as human beings continue to advance technology, metals will continue to play an essential role in their efforts.

And finally, as long as you keep in mind the fact that metals are responsive to extremes in emotion, and that extremes in emotion are a function of market conditions, you will do well. When emotions reign supreme, when traders and investors are in a frenzy, and when markets appear to be out of control, precious metals will be the preferred investments. Emotional markets are difficult to control or predict; however, these markets have established certain correlates over the years. One is the fact that metals will move as a result of emotional extremes. It is our job first to know this fact and then to use it to our advantage.

PROTECTING YOURSELF WITH INVESTMENTS IN RARE COINS (NUMISMATICS)

Investors can participate in the metals markets through the purchase and sale of coins. There are several ways to do this:

- *Bullion coins can be bought and sold through thousands of dealers the world over.* The value of these coins is determined by the value of the metal (bullion) and a broker's commission charge when bought and sold. Because commission charges can vary considerably, no specific percentage markup for commission can be given; however, 6 percent of the coin bullion value is common. In the case of special-issue coins, limited-production coins, or medals, there may be an additional premium above and beyond the bullion value of the coin itself. In such cases, the investor should take special considerations into account when making a decision about purchase. These will be discussed later on.

- *Numismatics, or rare coin collecting, is a highly specialized field with literally thousands of coin issues.* There are numerous considerations relating to the condition of coins that dramatically affect prices.

- *Since the mid-1980s, various firms have organized coin partnerships that manage investor funds in numismatic coins.* The influence of such partnerships has grown steadily as a function of the large amounts of money they control. Their effect on the market will continue to grow. Those who invest in numismatics should carefully consider the role of such large funds in affecting prices.

Now let's examine each of these alternatives in detail.

Bullion Coins

There are many different types of bullion coins to choose from. Although they are all essentially similar in terms of metal content, the differences among them are essentially aesthetic and price related. Coins such as South African Krugerrands, Canadian Maple Leafs, and Chinese Pandas are popular, but the primary reason for owning bullion coins is for their bullion value. Although you may see many advertisements touting the rarity of certain bullion coins, you must decide for yourself whether you are interested in numismatics or in bullion. If you are indeed interested in bullion, then virtually any bullion coin will do the job. Because there are so many different gold, silver, palladium, and platinum bullion coins, and so many more coming to market every year, it would be useless to discuss the various types of bullion coins you could buy. By the time this information has reached you, it will be outdated. I will give you some guidelines later on how to purchase bullion coins. As always, use the GIM approach described in Chapter 7.

Gold and Silver Bullion Coins

These are among the most popular and plentiful of the bullion coins. Remember that when you buy these, you will be paying for the metal content and broker commission, as well as sales tax in some cases. My advice is to shop around and compare prices before you buy, because commissions will vary considerably. You must also make certain that you are dealing with a reputable coin dealer. Be sure that you take possession of the coins you are buying. Through the years, many investors have been cheated by various schemes, all of which have involved delayed delivery to the buyer and/or holding coins for the customer.

Another factor to consider in buying gold bullion coins is liquidity. Eventually, there will come a time for you to sell your coins. You must be prepared to sell quickly, because market tops develop rapidly, and there can be substantial price swings when a top is reached. You should, therefore, accumulate the most

popular issues, because these will be the ones in greatest demand when the top is at hand.

It has been my experience that prices from one dealer to another can vary considerably during the time of a market top. I
urge you to compare prices when selling. You'll be surprised at
the different prices you'll be quoted. You may also be surprised
at the different prices you'll get for different quantities of coins,
often a better price for a larger quantity of coins.

Furthermore, I suggest that you do some research before selecting a coin dealer. There have been instances of forged bullion coins, and you are better off dealing with larger firms that
will stand behind the authenticity of the coins they sell. Don't be
afraid to ask questions about their policies; it's the only way
you'll find out what you need to know.

In buying silver bullion coins, remember that a much larger
quantity of silver bullion will need to be purchased, because the
price of silver as compared to gold is considerably smaller. A bag
of so-called junk silver, which consists of U.S.-circulated silver
coins, weighs about 45 pounds. For the same amount of money,
you can have eight to ten one-troy-ounce gold coins. This, of
course, raises the issue of storage for bullion coins, which will be
discussed later in this chapter.

Platinum and Palladium Bullion Coins

These coins are, in my opinion, the most interesting and
often the most attractive to collect. However, they are considerably less liquid and, therefore, more difficult to sell. There are
not too many platinum coin issues and even fewer palladium
issues. You can accumulate these, but make certain that there
will be a dealer who will buy them back from you when the time
comes. Prices could move dramatically higher, but the lack of a

liquid market will result in your not getting a good price when you want to sell. This is an important consideration, if you plan to profit from your investment.

Storing Bullion Coins

If you plan to accumulate a sizable position in bullion coins, you should be concerned about storage. And though some investors may choose to keep coins at home—perhaps under floorboards, in a mattress, in the freezer, or buried in the backyard—there are other ways to store your coins. The most common of these is to store your coins in bank safe-deposit boxes until you are ready to sell. Because these coins can be quite heavy and can take a large amount of space (particularly in the case of silver), you will need considerable space for a large quantity of bullion. It might be a good idea to keep boxes at a number of different banks.

Through the years, there has been much talk about the safety of items stored in bank safe-deposit boxes. Some feel that in the event of an emergency or banking crisis, you may not be given access to a bank's vault. If you are concerned about this, I suggest storing your bullion coins in a private vault not run by a bank or other financial institution. There are many such firms throughout the country, primarily in larger urban centers.

When to Buy Bullion Coins

Because bullion coins must be purchased for 100 percent cash (i.e., they cannot be bought on margin as with stocks and futures), you will want to accumulate your position slowly over a period of time. The best way to do this is by dollar cost averaging.

In other words, make regular purchases over an extended period of time well before the bottom of the market has been reached. By buying at lower and lower prices, you will slowly but surely average your cost down, and when the market begins its upswing, you will have accumulated a substantial position at a relatively low average cost. You could follow any of these strategies:

- Buy bullion coins monthly or weekly regardless of price, but make sure you do so when prices are relatively low or following a longer period of declines.

- Buy bullion coins only when prices are below a predetermined level.

- Buy coins on a scale-down basis only. Use the DCA strategy discussed in Chapter 9. In other words, buy only if the price is lower this time than it was the last time you bought.

- Buy more when prices are lower than they were the last time you bought. In other words, assume you bought one gold bullion coin at $397 last month and that the price this month is $347. You might decide to buy two coins. You could also determine a scale for every $25 or $50 increment below your original purchase price.

How to Shop for the Best Price

Although bullion coin prices are tied closely to the value of bullion, you'll be able to save money if you shop for your coins. Not only will you find the lowest commissions, but you may also find lower base prices for the coins. I suggest that you have between four to six sources each month, and that you contact them when you are ready to buy. Learn the price and then make your transactions. You can transact most of your business on the Internet, but follow all of the necessary precautions required in online financial transactions.

Selling your coins is a different matter. *You will want to sell your coins when prices are shooting ever higher.* It is always easiest to sell on the way up, and it is always easiest to buy on the way down. If you check with your dealers several times a day when prices are rising sharply, you'll see that prices can vary considerably. Accept the fact that you're not going to get the very top of a move, nor will you get the very bottom of a move. Be prepared to sell out your holdings more quickly than you accumulated them. Market bottoms can take weeks, often months, to develop, but market tops can happen in a matter of days. You will need to adjust your buying and selling strategies accordingly.

NUMISMATICS AND NUMISMATIC COIN INVESTMENT PROGRAMS

Numismatics offers tremendous potential to the skilled and patient investor, but it is a subject entirely unto itself. Some feel that this market offers the best of all worlds, because it combines rarity with the value of bullion. A study of the performance history of numismatics confirms this opinion, but investing profitably in numismatic coins is not a simple matter. I feel that all investors should own some numismatic coins, but the best way to do this is by enlisting the services of a professional dealer or expert, unless, of course, you have the time and skill necessary to make informed decisions.

As an alternative to collecting rare coins, you may turn your capital over to professional managers who will buy coins for you. Although the returns from some of these programs have been good, there are factors you should consider before you commit funds, such as the cost of commissions, management fees, experience of the managers, condition of the markets, and the details of the programs themselves.

Here are a few questions to ask before putting your money with a professionally managed coin fund:

- Are the commission charges reasonable?

- What are the management fees and/or incentive fees? Are they reasonable?

- What are the credentials of the program managers? Are they experienced numismatists?

- Has the firm had previous coin programs, and if so, what have been the results?

- Can you sell your interest at any time? If so, what are the details and charges? Are you locked in for a certain minimum length of time?

- How are the coins acquired? Are they bought at auction, or are they bought from the affiliated companies of the firm or from its directors? It is preferable that they be bought from sources other than the firm's managers or affiliated companies to avoid a conflict of interest.

- How will the coins be sold? Will they be sold at auction or privately placed? Coins sold at auction usually get better prices.

- Is there a loss-cutoff provision? In other words, will the program cease operations if net asset value drops below a given amount?

- Are there any other provisions for the protection of the investors?

- Is the fund registered properly with the appropriate state and/or federal agencies?

Consider carefully the answers to the above points, and before you take any action, consult with your attorney. Always ask for referrals from the firm, and don't do business with any individual or firm that you have not carefully checked first.

GUIDELINES FOR INVESTING IN COINS

Here is a synopsis of my guidelines and considerations regarding coins:

- Buying bullion coins is an excellent way for the new investor to get started in metals investing.

- Locate several coin dealers in your area or on the Internet and check prices regularly. You will come to know whose prices are the best, and whose commissions are the lowest.

- Be sure to check the credentials of numismatists, should you decide to enter this area of metals investing.

- Before you send funds to anyone for any program, investment plan, coins, or coin-related plans, check with your attorney or advisor.

- When you buy coins, do so on a dollar-cost-averaging basis. It is the most reasonable and sensible way of buying coins, and it will often help you get the best average purchase price.

- When you sell your bullion coins, be prepared to act much more quickly than when you bought the coins.

- Remember that market peaks come quickly, and that you will need to respond much more quickly than you did when you accumulated your position.

- Don't forget that liquidity is very important. If you have accumulated, or plan to accumulate, a large position in bullion coins, you must do so in coins that are easily liquidated.

- You can often save money by shopping for the best prices and the best commissions. Don't be afraid to negotiate with dealers, particularly if you are buying or selling larger quantities or if you have been a good customer.

- There is no need for you to pay a premium for special bullion-coin issues. If you want to collect coins, then do so as part of your numismatic portfolio; however, do not get this mixed up with your bullion-coin strategy.

- Such things as medals, commemoratives, proof coin sets, special issue coins, etc., are all items that will require you to pay a premium—often a healthy one. Do not confuse these with your bullion-coin purchase plan. Unless the market for these specialty items turns sharply higher, you will probably not recoup your original purchase price when you sell, particularly if you do not hold these items for a long time.

- The bullion-coin strategy is a slow and steady one ideal for long-term investors. You may accumulate coins for up to several years, while watching your dollars return either no profits or even shrink. This is normal, because market bottoms take a long time to develop. But keep in mind that your plan is designed to take advantage of the up market that will surely follow.

- There are many excellent coin dealers and coin advisory services that can be helpful as you make important investment decisions. Do a little research and find a service or advisor who can help you.

- Don't forget that storage is a significant problem, particularly in silver bullion coins. Make arrangements for storage that is both safe and accessible.

- When you see prices turn sharply higher, and when the situation appears to be incredibly positive, be prepared to liquidate some of your holdings, if not all of them, and be prepared to do so rather quickly.

While the information above has given you a general introduction to bullion coins as metals investments, it is by no means a complete coverage of the topic. Should you decide to put some of your funds into bullion and/or numismatic coins, I strongly suggest you do additional research along the guidelines provided in previous chapters.

FAST AND FURIOUS— THE HOTTEST GAMES IN TOWN

These games are reserved for only the most advanced players who have high disposable incomes and can benefit from higher risks. How do you know if you fit into this category? Chances are if you've gotten this far by investing, you don't need this book anymore. If you've gotten a good sum of money from Mom and Dad or grandparents, from the lotto, from winning a lawsuit, or from some other way, you need to read this book, because odds are you will be separated from your money quickly by the buck-feeding sharks who swim the financial waters in search of easy targets. Here are a few of the "hot games" and some precautions to consider:

■ *Trading the high-stakes futures markets.* Dos and don'ts of the bullion, bushels, and bales market. I have already given you information about this area earlier in this chapter. In advance, know that the vast majority of futures traders lose money. There are many reasons for this, the most significant of which is the fact that leverage in traditional futures is very high. Generally you pay for about 1 percent of the total value of your investment. This means that the price movements can be very large. Without a doubt, the futures markets are not for most investors. Be careful!

■ *Using a money manager to handle your futures trading account, yes or no?* The answer is yes and no. There are some money managers in the futures markets that have shown a fabulous performance history for several years. Such managers often give all the money back and then some. The best money manager for your futures trading account meets the following qualifications: (1) they have been in business for more than ten years; (2) they have shown profitable results at least 70 percent of the years that they have been managing money; (3) their "drawdowns" or losing periods have amounted to less than 30 percent of portfolio size; and (4) their management fees have not been excessive.

■ *Futures options trading—who makes the money in options?* Futures options trading is even more risky than futures trading. Generally, the futures options buyer is a loser most of the time. Some of the most outrageous schemes and scams in the markets have involved options trading. Because options have a limited life and lose value daily if the underlying market is not moving in the necessary direction, most options expire worthless. The investor loses all of his or her money and commission in such cases. On the other hand, the options seller makes money most of the time.

Therefore, if you can get into a reputable program of options selling, you will be better off than if you are only an options buyer. In addition, options strategies work much better than outright options buying.

■ *Stock options—covered options strategies to generate consistent profits.* This area has already been discussed. For futures options trading, stock options programs are more conservative.

■ *International stock markets—political risks make for large profit potential.* Trading and investing in foreign stock markets is a rapidly growing field. There are mutual funds, global asset funds, foreign currency funds, American depositary receipts (foreign stocks traded on U.S. exchanges), and world equity benchmark shares (WEBS) in which you invest in a basket of stocks in a given country. All of these are available and should be considered by the higher-tier investor.

■ *Foreign exchange (FOREX) trading—the good, the bad, and the ugly.* Be very careful about trading in the FOREX market. The lure is often that there are no commissions. That's the good news. The bad news is that you will be competing with banks and very large institutions. The markets are highly volatile and can bring you losses much faster than you can even imagine. I advise you to stay out unless you have $1 million in risk capital.

■ *Day trading in stocks and futures.* These are both viable areas for higher-tier investors as previously mentioned and detailed in this chapter.

■ *Hedge fund investing.* Hedge funds are more aggressive mutual funds that can buy and sell short stocks. They are not regulated by the government as closely or as aggressively as are traditional mutual funds. These funds are designed primarily for the larger investor, and many do not accept less than $100,000 as an initial investment. Since their performance can be highly volatile and variable, I suggest that you invest in what is called a Fund of Funds. This is a hedge fund that invests your money in a variety of hedge funds in order to even out the peaks and valleys in performance.

- *Single stock futures.* This area has already been discussed.

CHAPTER ELEVEN

STAYING AHEAD OF THE CURVE

Emerging Opportunities

What does the future have in store for investors? World economies are on the threshold of record growth. With the record growth will come myriad investment opportunities, particularly in emerging markets such as Eastern Europe, the Pacific Rim, and the former Soviet states. In addition to new markets, new technologies will offer investors some of the largest profit potentials since the early 1970s. Now is the time to plan for the future. Time passes all too quickly, and before we realize what has happened, another decade has passed and with it many profitable opportunities. This chapter will alert you to developing trends in world economies that can be your ticket to profits, early retirement, and wealth.

WHAT'S AHEAD IN THE AREA OF TECHNOLOGICAL BREAKTHROUGHS?

I have given you specific methods of investing and becoming financially independent. Recent studies support the finding that when economies make lows, there has also been a series of important technological breakthroughs. Assuming that this is indeed the case, and looking ahead to the next period of economic growth, here are my thoughts on what some of the breakthroughs might be. In my estimation, all of these will be prime areas for long-term investors and offer potentially large profits.

- *Genetic engineering and biotechnology are likely to be important areas of innovation.* These might prove to be the most profitable investment areas when the U.S. economy improves.

- *Routine space travel is likely to become a reality in the next 10 to 15 years.* This opens an entirely new era of transportation and exploration. The possibilities are virtually boundless.

- *Computer technology is changing dramatically.* Artificial intelligence, computers that learn from their mistakes, is growing rapidly. In the coming years, progress will come in quantum leaps. Recent innovations include so-called neural networks that can correct errors and actually learn. Computer technology will continue as a field of important innovation. Don't be surprised to see a marriage of genetic engineering and computer technology, resulting in a machine that can outperform the human brain many times over.

- *Alternative energy.* As conflict escalates in the Middle East, and as world needs for energy increase, the importance of

alternative energy development will increase. With this increase will come numerous investment possibilities. There
are a number of new companies in this field that offer considerable long-term growth potential.

- *Communications technology is due for some revolutionary changes.*
  Although advances in communications technology have
  been relatively stagnant for years, the coming economic
  boom may witness new developments using revolutionary
  methods and totally new technology.

- *Security and defense stocks and companies are likely to do well in
  the coming years.* Terrorist attacks all over the world are likely
  to continue and, in fact, may escalate in the next few years.
  Companies involved in security and defense are attractive,
  particularly in the area of Internet security.

It is important to keep in touch with areas of possibly new
technology in order to capitalize on them with your investment
dollars. Jay Forrester, the highly respected economist whose
computer-generated forecasts have been very accurate, com-
mented on innovations and the long-term economic cycle in an
interview with *Fortune* magazine in 1978. His words are as true
today as they were then. He was asked, "Do you have any idea of
the technological basis for the next major economic upturn?"

> I am no more sure of the shape of the next technologi-
> cal wave than other people. I expect that energy will
> move toward renewable and more decentralized sources,
> not only because of the nature of new energy sources,
> but because of changes in our social system. I expect that
> declining worldwide political stability with increasing un-
> rest and sabotage will combine with the persuasiveness of

decentralized energy sources—like solar and wind power and alcohol from farm products—to encourage decentralization. If individual countries can't understand and manage their economies, I doubt the likelihood of managing all countries simultaneously. (*Fortune,* 16 January 1978)

Again, I strongly suggest that you become an active reader of long-term forecasts generated by "futurists." The leading organization in this area is the World Future Society. You can learn more about them online at <www.wfs.org/futurist.htm>. Another good resource is *The Futurist,* which you can see online at <http://futurist.com>. Remember, what you learn about expectations will not be realities until they are confirmed by timing.

CHAPTER TWELVE

SUMMARY AND FINAL THOUGHTS

Before you venture off on your own, hopefully implementing some of my ideas and methods, I'd like to share with you some of my thoughts about the trends and patterns in economic cycles and some of my thoughts on investor psychology. First, let's deal with the psychology of investing.

A PERSPECTIVE ON INVESTOR PSYCHOLOGY

This is not the first book about long-wave economic cycles, nor will it be the last. Virtually every economist, investment advisor, or politician nowadays has his or her thoughts and opinions about what is and what's to come. As conditions become more volatile, and as reactions within the economic underpinnings are more pronounced, opinions and attitudes become more polarized. Although some experts believe that the long-wave cycles have their origin in the teachings and theories of various economists or philosophers, others claim that economic trends are random, unpredictable, and therefore, incapable of being effectively analyzed.

Still others believe that economic salvation is embodied in the virtues of the gold standard or in the seemingly rational policies of a balanced budget. Books, theories, opinions, and advice on this especially relevant subject are plentiful, but little concrete information is available that deals with the emotional aspects of investor behavior. Nor is there a confluence of opinion regarding the optimum methodology by which an investor or businessperson can implement specific investment strategies without the potentially destructive consequences of emotion, lack of discipline, fear, or greed.

For many years, advisors and economists have assumed that investors are reasonable, relatively normal, well-adjusted, nonneurotic, and self-disciplined individuals. Could it be that the opposite is true? Could so many investors and speculators be losers because they lack the necessary emotional prerequisites for investment success? Certainly, the experience of futures traders provides us with strong evidence that 80 to 90 percent of speculators in these markets tend to lose their starting capital. Could it be that the rate of losers is just as high in the stock market? Perhaps not. Perhaps only 50 percent of stock investors are net losers. Certainly, the percentage of losers is a direct function of the types of investments that are selected. It appears to me that a number of variables may either exacerbate losses or facilitate profits:

- The nonprofessional investor is likely to fare well in longer-term investments as opposed to shorter-term speculation.

- The investor who maintains a balanced portfolio is likely to fare better than the investor who puts all of his or her eggs in one basket. Diversification spreads risk and makes profitable results more likely.

■ Mutual fund investments appear to be the ideal area for a majority of investors inasmuch as they spread risk, diversify, and practice the discipline necessary for successful investing.

■ Investors with larger starting capital tend to do better in the long run inasmuch as they can diversify their holdings more quickly than can the individual beginning with limited capital.

■ The investor who is aware of his or her personal limitations, assets, and liabilities tends to fare better than the investor who plunges headlong into the markets without regard for the potential emotional consequences of his or her behavior.

■ Investors who follow a given plan or strategy tend to be successful more frequently than do those who place their money haphazardly or without regard to a given plan, system, or strategy.

■ Those who are capable of selling or selling short as well as buying tend to fare better than those who can trade only from the long side or are always bullish.

The fact that there are still losers in the stock and futures markets tends to negate the value of our purportedly great strides in business science and investment analysis. Computer technology, modern economic theory, and a veritable watershed of investment messiahs have not been able to make winners out of *all* of us. Facts and figures do not create investment winners unless they are implemented with discipline, consistency, and organization. I know from personal experience that strategy, theory, advice, analysis, trading systems, and investment schemes are only minor aspects of the success equation (although many would disagree with me).

J. Peter Steidlmayer, whose success in futures trading is known to few outside the field, has noted repeatedly that the formula for market profits is dependent on the discipline and emotional maturity of the trader. Although Steidlmayer was not the first to assert the importance of human emotion in the achievement of success, he did so in a concise and easily expressed fashion when he noted the following in *Markets and Market Logic* (Porcupine Press, 1986):

> Man's powers of observations are no longer crucial to his survival and thus have declined through underuse.
>
> Man's ability to think for himself analytically has also declined through lack of use. . . .
>
> Man as a class would prefer to be led and told what to do rather than think for himself. . . .
>
> Man as a class is inconsistent in his behavior: he will respond differently to the same situation and set of data depending on mood, stimuli, etc.

Although you may learn more about virtually all fields of investing from the many books available on this subject, you will find an obvious void in the area of investment psychology. One chapter in this book cannot erase the misconception that better investment methods will automatically lead to success. I do think that the analyses presented here of human psychology can provide valuable assistance to those who accept the notion that success does not immediately follow market understanding, unless it is accompanied by self-understanding and discipline.

A Question of Origin

There are those who contend that human behavior does not determine economic trends, and there are also those who argue in favor of economic determinism. Determinists claim that economic conditions result in stresses and strains that have a marked effect on human behavior and emotion. Poverty, for example, may breed frustration and aggression. Wealth may breed complacency and the need for more stimulation, which, in turn, may promote alcoholism or drug dependency as well as anxiety and psychophysiological responses such as ulcers and migraines.

On the other hand, psychologists may argue that emotion influences economic behavior. Their line of reasoning might be stated as follows:

> Human emotional responses such as anxiety and stress produce the need for such things as liquor consumption, movie watching, and overindulgence in food. Such activities are compensatory or defensive mechanisms that are inspired by psychological needs. Insecurity, for example, may stimulate certain types of economic behavior, such as the accumulation of material possessions, as a form of compensation. Irrational fear may cause investors to liquidate stocks, futures contracts, real estate, collectibles, and the like, thereby causing market crashes. Insatiable greed may stimulate excessive buying of stocks and other investments regardless of price and regardless of potential return.

Each of these positions is deterministic, however. They are unacceptable lines of reasoning. They take an extremely narrow view of humankind. These positions fail to consider the fact that human behavior is composed of inputs from all of the senses and virtually every aspect of the environment. Just as emotion and psychology alone cannot be seen as the stimulus of economic activity, we cannot view economic activity as the sole cause of human behavior and emotion.

Some theorists have claimed that the fundamental basis of economic activity is war. Yet such a narrow interpretation is also faulty. Life, economics, history, and systems are neither simple nor readily relegated to constant causes. Whereas one economic cycle may have been precipitated by a given event or events of specific origin, another cycle may have been precipitated by entirely different causes.

Some theorists have claimed that the origin of long-wave cycles rests in technological breakthroughs. I find these assertions equally fallacious. In reality, economic and investment behavior arises from a multiplicity of inputs—some psychological, some economic, some technological, some sociological, some religious, and so forth.

Economic Trends

This is an important area of consideration, because it will likely affect all of your investments, whether in stocks, futures, options, or real estate. Consider some of my random thoughts about history and the big-picture outlook, for you as an investor and for the economy in general.

Instant Gratification

Immediacy reigned supreme in the 1990s and continues today. You can log onto the Internet and within seconds can see world news; download music and video chips; chat with people you've never met; post bulletins in newsgroups; buy books, videos, or CDs for delivery the next day; find a new or used car; and even buy software for immediate downloading. For those who seek to satisfy their sexual desires, no matter what time of day, thousands of porn Web sites are available for instant access at the mere entry of a credit card number.

On the more pragmatic side of things, you can trade stocks online with instant electronic order entry, you can check your bank balance, transfer funds, or donate money to your favorite charity. And if none of this happens fast enough for you with a 56K modem, you can connect using a high-speed connection, a superfast TI line, or a variety of high-speed alternatives. And you can enjoy all of these on your new incredibly fast computer that sports an ultrafast CD-ROM drive with a fast access internal hard drive. Of course, your pleasure and speed of processing can be increased with a few gigabytes of high-speed memory chips and a voice recognition package designed to speed up inputs. And, of course, you can relax in style as you do all of this on new office furniture you don't have to make payments on for 12 months and at the low, low rate of 3 percent guaranteed.

Speed has pervaded virtually every aspect of life. Stocks move up and down faster than ever before. News travels across the world instantly via the Internet.

ECONOMIC YIN AND YANG: CYCLES OF BOOM AND BUST

Cycles of boom and bust are not new to world economies or stock markets. There have been at least six major boom and bust cycles in America, and many more minor cycles. A study of economic history underscores the inescapable fact that markets and economies breathe in and must eventually breathe out. Markets rise and fall, often in relatively predictable rhythms. When markets are in an upward trend, optimism reigns supreme. Politicians are elated, the public is happy, investment managers are proud, and retirees find little to complain about as long as their monies have been wisely invested.

Ultimately, as the momentum of good times grows, optimism reaches a state of euphoria that frequently culminates in a climactic buying surge. More often than not, such extreme levels of buying and optimism correlate closely with an end to the period of "boom." Whereas the future looked bright during the period of boom, and perhaps brightest at its peak, events and investor psychology soon change with the changing tide of the markets and the economy.

When the cycle of bust begins, optimism is still high. Shortly after a few severe declines in the stock market, as well as a few negative indications from government, pessimism begins to spread. Markets decline, the economy contracts, and politicians fear for their jobs. The public is angry, shocked, and frustrated that the markets are declining. Money managers are fearful of speculative stocks and begin to seek conservative investments for their clients. Retirees are frustrated as they watch the value of their stock portfolio erode almost daily. Pessimism breeds more pessimism until the stock market and the overall economy plunge even lower in a last gasp of selling. At times, only a whimper and not a bang characterize the end of a "bust" phase. Occasionally, a new boom cycle is born of humble beginnings following a period of stagnation, one during which there is relatively little movement but during which markets and economies gather energy for the coming upward phase.

Can Government Make a Difference?

Investors are encouraged to have faith in the ability of governments to control boom and bust cycles. After all, governments can control the supply of money, interest rates, the degree of market speculation, fiscal policies that affect supply and demand, credits and loans to foreign countries, as well as a host of other less-significant variables. All of these, when combined, theoretically exert a major effect on the direction of stocks, other investments, and the general economy. But are they really effective?

Students of American history point to the fact that economic depressions during the terms of Presidents Van Buren, Buchanan, Grant, Cleveland, Theodore Roosevelt, and Woodrow Wilson were either allowed to occur due to government disinterest or were exacerbated by the fact that none of these administrations took an active role in avoiding or alleviating them. On the other hand, the Hoover administration parted with the tradition, taking an active role in economic policies designed to overcome the severe effects of the Great Depression. And this marked a turning point in the role of government with regard to economic health, safety, and welfare.

Today, government is actively involved in facilitating economic growth, controlling inflationary pressures, stimulating the economy when necessary, and hopefully, minimizing the effects of boom and bust cycles. The prevailing opinion among investors is that the government not only has a large arsenal of weapons to use in the fight against economic extremes, but also that the weapons will work when they are needed. This, of course, remains to be seen. Ultimately, no matter what governments may do, the individual investor alone is responsible for his or her own successes and failures.

Boom and Bust Cycles

The cycles of boom and bust in free world economies are not nearly as predictable as are the oscillations of planets, the motion of electrons, or the coming and going of the seasons. However, they do have their internal and external patterns, which within a reasonable degree of variation have shown a lengthy history of repetition. A number of well-respected classical economists, including such notables as Joseph Schumpeter, recognized this fact, incorporating it into their theories of prices and economics. For your own enlightenment, you may want to read the writings of theorists such as Keynes, Schumpeter, Kitchins, and Kondratieff.

Good Guys versus Bad Guys

Stock and commodity price history in America reads like a drama of good guys versus bad guys. The good guys in this high-states economic thriller are the bulls, the optimists, those who feel that markets will rise forever with only minor setbacks along the way. They are the politicians who have "worked hard" to improve the lot of their constituents. They are the mutual fund managers who have practiced their analytical skills, choosing the best stocks that money can buy. And, they are the bankers who in their endless beneficence have lent money to individuals and businesses, thereby allowing them to profit in a growing economy.

In their overly optimistic view, all is for the best in the best of all possible markets. Declines are seen as "corrections." Bad news is considered an opportunity to buy more stocks. "Buy high and sell higher" is one of their credos. "Buy low and sell high" is their theme. Government attempts to control the economy from excessive growth are a necessary but bitter pill to swallow, yet government in this phase of growth is considered a necessary evil. Yes, even the government is seen favorably when the economy is healthy and stocks are rising.

Those who are cautious, pessimistic, or bearish are the bad guys. They are often labeled as the "gloom and doomers." Their view is that upward price moves are temporary, that sooner or later markets will crash in a syncope of bad news. In their pessimistic view, all progress is temporary. They view economic statistics as lies perpetuated by a government whose sole purpose is to hide the economic truth from the people they were elected to serve. They promote "hard money" investments as a hedge against the eventual collapse of stocks, systems, and government.

The good guys and bad guys are not organized into definitive camps, clubs, or groups, but they are everywhere. Every nation, every economy, every political party, and every school of economic theory has its share of the yin and yang. While there are elements of truth in each camp, the actual truth is likely to be found somewhere in the middle. A good guy can become a bad guy almost instantly, depending on his or her view of the markets and the economy. Conversely, changing his or her opinions from negative to positive can redeem a bad guy. Clearly, at the peak of a market and at the top of an economic cycle, good guys substantially outnumber bad guys. And at the end of an economic cycle or declining market, bad guys are in the majority, while good guys are afraid to come "out of the closet."

MARKETS HAVE A LIFE OF THEIR OWN

The more we learn about markets and economies, the more we realize that they have a life of their own. They are born, often from the ashes of a previously moribund economy, and they grow slowly at first. They continue to grow until they reach a crest and then begin to decline. Their fall is at first unnoticeable, perhaps even insipid. However, as the decline continues, it gains momentum under the forces of economic gravity, and eventually a rapid decline ensues. Ultimately, the decline slows, a period of consolidation follows, and a bottom is eventually reached.

The life cycle of markets and economies follows the same general phases, although the ramifications of each phase are different. Clearly, a secular change in the economic trend can have a domino effect on all sectors of the economy, including the stock and commodity markets. Yet, it is also possible for the stock and commodity markets to affect the economic trend in certain circumstances. This "chicken or egg" question has long been a source of controversy among economists, market technicians, traders, investors, market analysts, bankers, and government. The ultimate answer will never be known, because any market or economy functions in a vacuum. An excess of negative economic news can put fear into the hearts of investors and investment managers. Their attitudes can change as a result of perceived fundamentals, which in turn may prompt them to sell. Mass negative perceptions may result in an avalanche of selling that will, in turn, cause security prices to decline.

On the other hand, the overall economic outlook may be positive; however, concerted selling of stocks by large investors and traders can reverberate through the economy, causing investors to avoid stocks, cut back on spending, and thereby affect the overall economy. Clearly, the interrelationships of all economic sectors, news, emotion, stock market trends, and international and domestic news all operate in a complex fashion that maintains an often delicate balance.

YESTERDAY, TODAY, AND TOMORROW

The last stock market rally started in the early 1980s. On a very broad scale, plotting stock trends using a logarithmic measure, the rally actually began in 1932 following the Great Depression. There have only been a handful of significant declines since the start of the greatest bull market in history. Beginning in 1995, the U.S. stock market started a near vertical acceleration. While there are numerous comparisons between the current U.S. stock market and the stock market of the 1920s, there are more dissimilarities than similarities.

A simple conclusion that the U.S. stock market is destined to crash based on similarities between the stock market in 2000 and the pre-1929 crash market alone is likely to be wrong as well as unrealistic. However, there are other causes for concern, causes that are global, interrelated, and considerably more significant than any aspects of the U.S. or world economies of the 1920s. These concerns cause stocks to decline and in so doing cause opportunities for long-term investors to buy quality stocks.

Paper Millionaires

The largest bull market in U.S. history created more paper millionaires than any stock market rally heretofore. The largest bull market in U.S. history attracted more investment dollars into mutual funds than has any other market in U.S. history. And the stock market rally lulled more investors into a false sense of security than any market in U.S. history. Now that the bull market has ended, erasing trillions of dollars in paper profits, the time is right and ripe for new investors to step into the picture. And this is where you come in. This is where the present book and my methods will be your best friends.

If you have learned your lessons well, you are now prepared to embark on a moneymaking venture and adventure. If, however, you have not comprehended what I have presented, I urge you to go back and reread this book.

SUMMING UP THE LESSONS LEARNED

Here is a general summary of what I have taught you in this book. If any of these points is unfamiliar or unclear to you, go back and review them.

- You can be your own financial expert.

- The General Investment Model (GIM) gave you the basic approach to how your plan for financial independence can be implemented.

- The Setup-Trigger-Follow-Through (STF) approach showed you how an expectation turns into an investment.

- The dollar cost averaging, or DCA, method in its several forms showed you how to fund your investments.

- The momentum method (MOM) of stock selection showed you how to time your market entry.

- My portfolio recommendations showed you how to put your ideas and money to work in the markets.

KEEP IN TOUCH

Jake Bernstein and MBH Commodity Advisors, Inc.
P.O. Box 353
Winnetka, IL 60093
Phone: 847-446-0800
Fax: 847-446-3111
E-mail: Jake@trade-futures.com
Web sites: www.trade-futures.com
www.2chimps.com

PRACTICE CHARTS AND ANALYSES

If you are truly interested in learning my MOM method for selecting stocks that have the potential to make large moves, you will want to take the following practice charts and lessons seriously. I suggest following these three steps for each chart:

1. Make several copies of the practice charts that follow.

2. Read the assignment that accompanies each chart and follow the instructions.

3. Consult the answer chart and check your work.

The key to effective stock selection using the MOM method is practice.

PRACTICE CHARTS

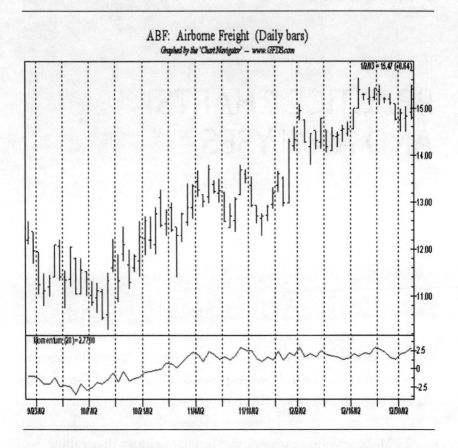

ABF: Airborne Freight (Daily bars)
Graphed by the 'Chart Navigator' – www.GFDS.com

Practice Chart 1 There is a MOM buy signal on this chart. Can you find it? What happened after the buy signal? Where would you have bought this stock based on the buy signal?

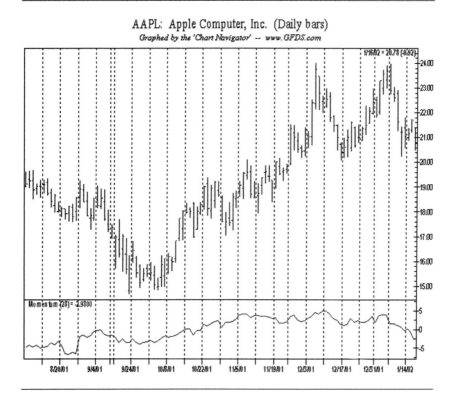

AAPL: Apple Computer, Inc. (Daily bars)
Graphed by the 'Chart Navigator' -- www.GFDS.com

Practice Chart 2 Can you spot the signal or signals on this chart? Were they buy or sell signals? Was there more than one signal? What happened after the signal or signals? What is the current condition of this stock? Is it about to give a new signal?

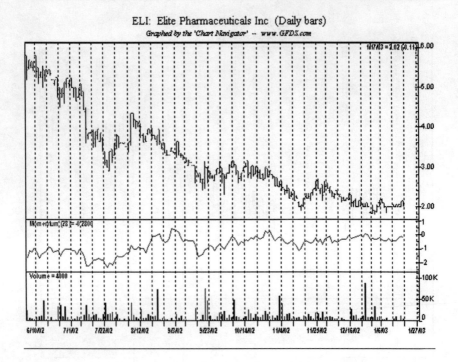

ELI: Elite Pharmaceuticals Inc (Daily bars)

Graphed by the 'Chart Navigator' -- www.GFDS.com

Practice Chart 3 Can you spot the signal or signals on this chart? Were they buy or sell signals? Was there more than one signal? What happened after the signal or signals? Is trading volume an issue? What is the current condition of this stock? Is it about to give a new signal? Is there something about this stock that might have prevented you from investing in it?

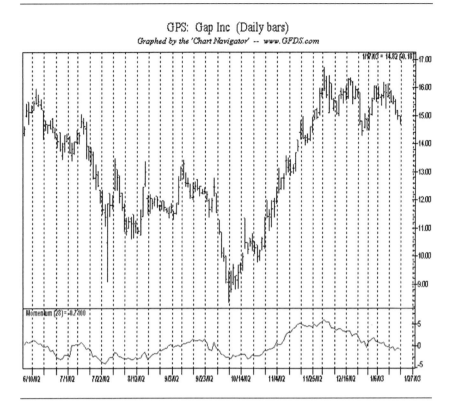

GPS: Gap Inc (Daily bars)

Graphed by the 'Chart Navigator' -- www.GFDS.com

Practice Chart 4 Can you spot the signal or signals on this chart? Were they buy or sell signals? Was there more than one signal? What happened after the signal or signals? What is the current condition of this stock? Is it about to give a new signal?

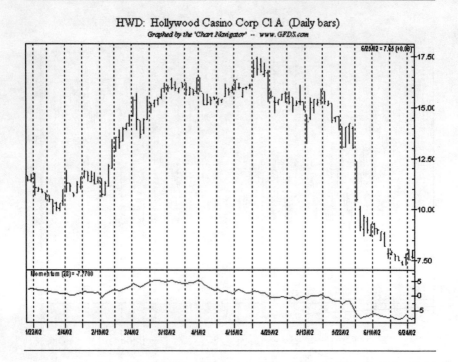

HWD: Hollywood Casino Corp Cl A (Daily bars)
Graphed by the 'Chart Navigator' -- www.GFDS.com

Practice Chart 5 Can you spot the signal or signals on this chart? Was there a good indication that this stock was destined to top? Can you find the sell signal? Were there other signals? What happened after the signal or signals? What is the current condition of this stock? Is it about to give a new signal?

ANSWERS TO PRACTICE CHARTS

Here are the answers to the practice charts. Take your time and carefully read my commentary and analysis.

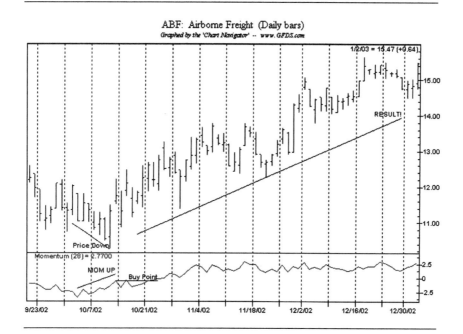

ABF: Airborne Freight (Daily bars)
Graphed by the 'Chart Navigator' -- www.GFDS.com

Practice Chart 1: Analysis The chart shows price making a new low in October, while MOM did not make a new low. Thereafter, the BUY POINT was penetrated and the stock would have been bought. The result was higher prices. Although MOM has not moved appreciably higher, there has been no MOM sell signal and, assuming you followed the rules, you would still be in this stock with a stop loss to manage your profit.

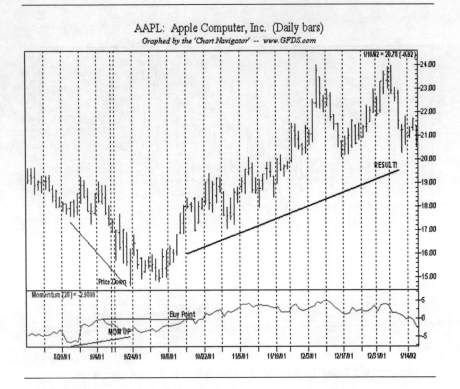

AAPL: Apple Computer, Inc. (Daily bars)
Graphed by the 'Chart Navigator' -- www.GFDS.com

Practice Chart 2: Analysis The chart shows price making a new low, while momentum was moving higher. This was a setup for the buy point, which was triggered in October. A move to higher prices followed, as you can see by my notes on the chart. As of the end of this chart, prices were making new highs, while momentum was moving lower, setting up a sell signal.

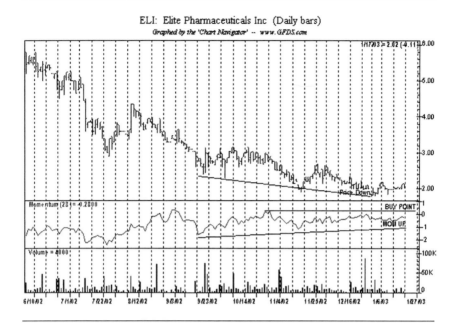

ELI: Elite Pharmaceuticals Inc (Daily bars)
Graphed by the 'Chart Navigator' -- www.GFDS.com

Practice Chart 3: Analysis The chart shows price moving lower, while momentum is moving higher. This has set up a potential buy signal. However, there is a problem. As you can see, the trading volume (number of shares traded daily) is very low. And this could be problematic. The low volume would cause me to stay out of this stock.

GPS: Gap Inc (Daily bars)
Graphed by the 'Chart Navigator' -- www.GFDS.com

Practice Chart 4: Analysis The chart shows price moving lower for a lengthy period of time, while momentum was moving higher. This set up a buy point, which was penetrated and yielded a buy signal. The result was higher prices. Currently, price and MOM are moving lower, which is a normal situation. Based on the signals, the investor who owns this stock would be using a stop loss to lock in a profit in the event that the stock declines.

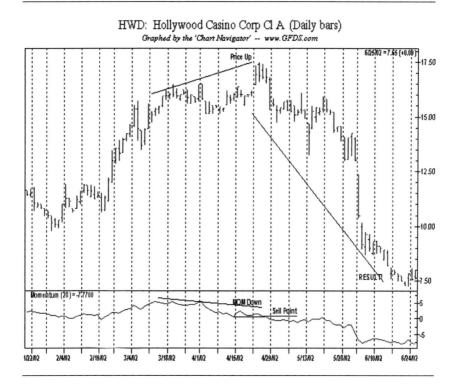

HWD: Hollywood Casino Corp Cl A (Daily bars)
Graphed by the 'Chart Navigator' -- www.GFDS.com

Practice Chart 5: Analysis The chart shows price making a new high, while MOM was moving lower. This was a setup for a sell signal at the indicated sell point. As you can see from the chart, the stock declined sharply and currently remains in a declining trend with no indication of a bottom as yet.

A considerable amount of investment information is available on-line and at no charge via the Internet. Here are some places you can visit to get valuable information on investing, as well as price quotations and the momentum indicator. Some of these sites are *not* free, so be careful what you sign up for.

Price Quotations and Timing Indicators (Including Momentum)

www.barchart.com

www.futuresource.com

www.gfds.com

www.stockcharts.com

General Investment Information on Stocks and Futures

www.bonds-online.com (an excellent resource for bond investing)

www.cnbc.com (for news, interviews, and price updates)

www.dripcentral.com (for information on dividend reinvestment programs)

www.invest-faq.com (for general investment information)

http://investorsleague.com/index.html (for practice and information on trading)

www.ipmi.org (for news and inflation on precious metals)

www.maketocracy.com (become a mutual fund manager with play money)

www.morningstar.com (for mutual fund information)

http://networth.quicken.com (for mutual fund information)

http://quote.yahoo.com (for news, information, and resources)

www.stocksmart.com (for general information on stocks)

www.trade-futures.com (for futures trading information)

www.2chimps.com (for short-term and day trading information)

www.yardeni.com (sometimes a little radical but a good information source on stocks and economic forecasts, trends, etc.)

INDEX

A

Action, 49, 87–89, 91, 92
  momentum and, 114
  premature, 93–94
Alternative energy, 178–79
Analysis paralysis, 49
Analysts, 28, 68–70
Analytical thinking, 184
Artificial intelligence, 178
Art of the Deal, The (Trump), 91
Attitude, realistic, 52

B

Bearish divergence, 113, 114–17
Beat the Millennium Crash (Bernstein), 160
Bernstein, Elliott, 10, 101
Bernstein, Jake, 4–10, 101, 106, 121, 136, 137, 160, 194
Biased expert, 104
Blind trust, 41
Brokerage analysts, 68–70
Brokerage scandals, 28, 63, 104
Bullion coins, 163–72
Bullish divergence, 113, 114–17
Business publications, 72–73
Buying orders, 47
Buy signal, 117

C

Capital, starting, 24, 58–59, 90–91, 183
Charts, practice, 121–28, 195–205
Children, 25–26
  financial issues and, 38–40, 76–77
  investment research and, 43
  whole life insurance and, 37
CNBC analysts, 69–70
Coins and precious metals, 159–72
  gold and silver bullion, 164–65
  investment programs, 168–70, 168–72
  liquidity of, 164, 171
  platinum and palladium bullion, 165–66
  protecting yourself with, 162–63
  shopping for price, 167–68
  storing, 166, 172
  strategy, 161
  when to buy, 166–67
College expenses, 39–40, 76–77
Commitment, 23, 25–26
Commodity trading, 8, 190–91
Communications technology, 179
Computer(s)
  investment and, 29–30
  neural networks, 178
  technology, 178
Confirmation, 87
  see also Timing method
  momentum and, 114
Consistency, 26–27
Contrary opinion, 14–15
Covered option writing, 158

D

Day trading, 119, 138, 159, 174
Defense stocks/companies, 179
Detachment, 52
Determinism, 186–87
Discipline, 46, 51, 54, 65, 184

Disposable income, 77
Divergence, 109, 113–17
Diversification, 17, 31, 182–83
Dividend reinvestment programs
  (DRIPs), 151
Dollar cost averaging, 60, 146–51, 154
  bullion coins and, 167, 172
  mutual funds and, 146
  by price, 147–49
  by time, 149–51
Dollar risk stops, 121
Dow Jones Industrial stocks, 148

E

Economic cycles, 11, 187–91
  boom and bust cycles, 190
  government and, 189
  origin of trends, 185–86
  stock/commodity price history and,
    190–91
Economic determinism, 185–86
Education expenses, 39–40, 76–77
Emerging markets, 177–80
Emotion, investment and, 60, 184
  detachment, 52
  fear and greed, 185
  self-knowledge, 45–54
Energy, alternative, 178
Expectation, 13, 84–87, 114

F

Fear, 46, 185
Financial advisors/planners, 74–75,
  159
Financial goals, 24–25, 55–79
  financial freedom, 135–37
  losses and, 58
  setting realistic/attainable, 77–78
  skills and, 64–66
  starting rules, 64–73
Ford Motor Company, 150
Forecasts, 47
Foreign exchange (FOREX) trading,
  174
Foreign stock markets, 174
Forrester, Jay, 179

Franchises, 70
Fund of funds, 175
Futures/futures options, 8, 137,
  140–41, 159, 173–74
Futures traders, 182
Futurists, 180

G

Gambling, 129–30, 131–32, 137–38
General Electric, 150
General Investment Model (GIM),
  81–100
  action, 87–89, 114
  confirmation, 87, 101, 114
  expectation, 85–87, 114
  flow chart, 83
  historical pattern, 84–85, 113–14
  management, 89–90, 114
  method. *See* Timing method
  planning for the future using,
    90–92
  setup, trigger, and follow-through,
    92–99, 116
  summary, 99–100
Genetic engineering, 178
Gold, 86, 97–99, 164–65
Granville, Joe, 60
Great Depression, 189
Greed, 46, 61, 185

H

Hedge fund investing, 174–75
Historical patterns, 11–12, 84–85
  momentum and, 113–14
*How to Trade the New Single Stock
  Futures* (Bernstein), 106, 136

I

Impulse, 46
Income, disposable, 77
Inflation, 160
Insiders, 47–48
Instant gratification, 132, 186–87
Internal Revenue Service, 42
International stock markets, 174

Internet
   businesses, 56
   references/resources, 30, 75–76,
      120, 153, 155, 180, 207–8
   security, 179
Intraday charts, 119
Investing in Metals (Bernstein), 160
Investment
   advisors, 67–70
   asset protection, 40–42
   children and, 38–40
   computers and, 30
   investor types, 129
   management, 89–90
   marriage issues, 33–38, 42–43
   methods/accuracy/risk, 108
   outdated ideas for, 27–29
   partnerships, 22–23
   plan/strategy, 183
   preparation checklist, 23–31
   pressure and, 30–31
   real estate as, 139–40
   selection/timing of, 102–5
   shoestring budget. *See* Shoestring-
      budget investments
   significant capital and, 157–75
   stock market and, 138
   success factors, 51–53
   vehicles, 136–37
Investor psychology/behavior, 45–54,
   181–87
   economic determinism, 185–86
   economic trends and, 186
   emotions and, 184
   instant gratification and, 186–87
   profit/loss variables, 182–83
   successful investment factors, 51–53

J–K

Jackson, Michael, 143–44
KISS, 16

L

Leverage, 136, 140
Life insurance, 35–37
Livermore, Jesse, 8

Living trust, 41
Losses, 13, 48–49, 50, 58–63, 59, 134
   riding, 60
   variables that exacerbate, 182–83

M

*McKay's Extraordinary Popular Delusions
   and the Madness of Crowds,* 15
Market
   divergence/changes in trend,
      113–17
   life cycles, 191–93
   momentum and, 112
   timer, 104–5
Markets and Market Logic
   (Steidlmayer), 184
Marriage, and investment, 33–40,
   42–43
   children and, 38–40
   life insurance considerations,
      35–37
   tax considerations, 37–38
   two-income families, 34–35
MBH Commodity Advisors Inc., 194
Mechanical methods, 51
Momentum, 109–12
   calculating, 111–12
   divergence/changes in trend,
      112–17
   market indications and, 112
   normal conditions for, 110–11
Momentum Stock Selection (Bernstein),
   106, 121, 158
morningstar.com, 155
Moving average, 149
Mutual funds, 28, 136, 146, 183
   children and, 38
   dividend reinvestment programs
      and, 151, 152, 154
   load *vs.* no-load funds, 154–55

N–O

Neural networks, computer, 178
Numismatics, 163, 168–70. *See also*
   Coins and precious metals
Offshore trust, 41

Online businesses, 56
Online references/resources, 30, 75–76, 120, 153, 155, 180, 207–8
Organization, 26–27, 62
Overtrading, 51

P

Palladium bullion coins, 165–66
Partnerships, 22–23, 27
Patterns, historical, 11–12, 84–85
Persistence, 52, 64–65
Platinum bullion coins, 165–66
Practice timing charts, 195–205
    analysis of, 200–205
Precious metals. *See* Coins and precious metals
Price, buy/sell behavior and, 48
Profit in the Futures Markets! (Bernstein), 137
Profits, 134, 182–83
Pro forma earnings projections, 72–73
Publications, 72–73
Pure trust, 41

R

Rate of Change (ROC), 112
Real estate, 13, 139–40
References/resources online, 30, 74–75, 120, 153, 155, 180, 207–8
Reminiscences of a Stock Operator (Lefèvre), 8
Revocable trust, 41
Risk/risk management, 19–21, 121
Rumors, 60–61, 70–71, 95–96

S

Scale investing/scale trading, 147
Sector expert, 105
Security stocks/companies, 179
Self-control, 65–66
Self-discipline, 65
Self-employment, 56
Self-knowledge, 45–54
Selling orders, 47

Sell signal, 118
Setup, 93–94
Setup, trigger, and follow-through (STF), 92–99, 116
    examples, 93–96
    gold and, 97–99
    model of, 97
Shoestring-budget investments, 143–55
    dividend reinvestment programs, 151, 154
    dollar cost averaging, 146–51, 154
    portfolio suggestions, 154–55
Short-term trading, 158
Simple trust, 40
Simplicity, 16
Single stock futures, 136, 157–58
Space travel, 178
Standard and Poor's
    500 index, 148
    futures cycle chart, 4-year, 85
Starting capital, 24, 58–59, 90–91, 183
Steidlmayer, J. Peter, 184
Stock(s), 136
    bargain, 59
    covered option writing, 158
    foreign stock market, 174
    price history, 190–91
    single stock futures, 157–58
Stock Market Strategies That Work (Bernstein and Bernstein), 10, 101, 106
Stock options, 136, 159, 174
Stock picker, 105
Stone, W. Clement, 144
Stop loss, 121, 153
Strategy, 183

T

Tax considerations, 37–38, 75
Technical analysis, 158
Technology, 177–79
Term insurance, 36–37
Timing method, 12–13, 68, 101–28
    analysis, 200–205
    divergence/changes in trend, 113–17

introducing, 106–8
momentum, 109–12, 120
practice, 120–28, 195–205
selection/timing of investments,
  102–5
signal, 117–19
Tips, 60–61, 70–71
Trend follower, 104
Trump, Donald, 91
Trusts, 40–42

W–Z

WEBS, 174
Whole life insurance, 35–36
World equity benchmark shares
  (WEBS), 174
World Future Society, 180
Wright-Hargreaves, 7
Y2K hysteria, 14, 86–87
zacks.com, 155